Who Do You Say You Are?

George A. Maloney, S.J.

LIVING FLAME PRESS
325 RABRO DRIVE, HAUPPAUGE, NY 11788

Who Do You Say You Are?

George A. Maloney, S.J.

All rights reserved. This book or any part thereof must not be reproduced in any form without permission of the publisher.

Published by:
Living Flame Press/325 Rabro Drive/Hauppauge, N.Y. 11788

ISBN: 0-914544-64-0

Copyright©1986 George A. Maloney, S.J.
Printed in the United States of America

Dedication

To Dolores Harrison who is a survivor.

TABLE OF CONTENTS

Introduction	1
Chapter One: Who Do You Say You Are?	7
Chapter Two: Obedience, Love and Freedom	19
Chapter Three: Ascension	31
Chapter Four: God Speaks to Us in Dreams	43
Chapter Five: The Spirit Dwells Within You	53
Chapter Six: Living the Mass	65
Chapter Seven: Finding God in All Things	77
Chapter Eight: Prayer With Your Whole Being	89
Chapter Nine: Stress, Inner Peace and Healing	101
Chapter Ten: Contemplation and Self-Emptying Love	111
Chapter Eleven: Eucharist	121

INTRODUCTION

A modern French contemplative and social worker among the poor and alienated of Parisian society, Madeleine Delbrêl, wrote: "God weighs more than all the world put together!" The writer is not opposing God against the world and encouraging us to choose Him over all of God's creatures.

She is giving voice to modern men and women in their desperate, yet seemingly pathetic longing for perfect Beauty that transcends all other limited, created beauty. It is the deepest desire that gnaws at the center of our being for the "Unpossessable" that makes all other possessions vain as the poet, Francis Thompson, writes.

God alone is great, beautiful, powerful, the Source of all being. Yet He can never be separated from us and the created world. He is love (1 Jn 4:8) and love is always self-emptying. Love does not merely give gifts or created things to the beloved. Love wishes to be a gift of self to the other. Love can never be satisfied with any other communication which does not move to unending ever-increasing communion where the Lover and the Beloved become each other in deepest, ongoing union. Yet in this union of oneness, both the *I* and the *Thou* are birthed into their unique personhood.

God's Glory Incarnate

The good news that Jesus, the Word made flesh and dwelling among us (Jn 1:14), came to reveal to us is that God is not far away from us, but ". . . it is in him that we live, and move, and exist" (Ac 17:28). He comes to reveal to us God's greatness and glory. ". . . and we saw his glory, the glory that is his as the only Son of the Father, full of grace and truth" (Jn 1:14).

Moses begged Yahweh to show Himself to him. "Show me your glory, I beg you" (Ex 33:18). But Yahweh told Moses it was impossible to see Him and live. Yet God has given us His Son in whom we can see the awesome glory and transcendent beauty of God. "Here is a place beside me. You must stand on the rock, and when my glory passes by, I will put you in a cleft of the *rock*, and shield you with my hand while I pass by" (Ex 33:22).

Who Are You?

This book is made up of eleven inter-related chapters. They serve as the purpose of this book to lead you, the reader, into a God-given answer and experience through faith, hope and love to the fundamental question all of us human beings are daily being asked by God, Trinity: "Who do you say you are?"

For the Christian disciple of Jesus, already initiated into a loving relationship of immanence with the risen Lord dwelling within her/him, there can be no ultimate answer to this basic question except through God's revelation in and through Jesus Christ. Modern psychology, philosophy, sociology, anthropology or any other science of perceptual knowledge can never fully bring us to an adequate answer.

The answer can not be merely an answer bound by the limitations of our own human understanding. It is to be discovered as we experience the answer to the most primary question we are always invited to respond to in faith, the question Jesus asked those whom He met on earth during His public preaching. And He still at each moment of our lives asks this of you and me. "Who do you say I am?"

The Spirit Reveals Who Christ Is

When we reflect upon the interior forces that motivate us in our choices of why we think, do and say what we do each moment of our lives, we see ourselves as a bundle of "selves." Which is our true self? God made us, male and female, according to His own image and likeness which is Jesus Christ (Gn 1:26-27).

It is only by the Holy Spirit that you and I can understand our true selves in the intimate oneness He brings about with Jesus Christ, the risen Lord, both God and man, who leads us to the Father. This same Spirit speaks to us of the "not-yet" through our dreams.

God's Spirit of love who proceeds both from the Father and the Son, leads us into God's true love which is given us (Rm 5:5). This experienced love of the triune God dwelling within us is manifested by the level of obedience, love and freedom we show in our daily living as we seek always to return God's love by the gift of our love to God and to neighbor.

A Book of Prayer

This book, therefore, deals with prayer. It is not primarily concerned with "saying prayers," yet this also is a part of true Christian prayer. It seeks to lead the reader into a contemplative state of *being prayer* toward God at all times. It is "to pray incessantly" as St. Paul exhorts us (1 Th 5:18).

Thus we seek in one chapter to find out how we can pray holistically with our whole being. Another chapter deals with obstacles to our wholeness in Christ, emphasizing especially the factor of stress as destructive and the healing of such "unhealth" and lack of harmony through contemplative prayer.

Kenotic Love

Contemplative prayer as a state of being in our true self in Christ unfolds out of God's revelation of Jesus Christ as the *kenosis*, or self-emptying love of the Trinity made manifest in our history as suffering and dying Servant of Yahweh.

Experiencing God's self-emptying love working for us and with us in each moment of our earthly existence, we have the means to live contemplatively by finding God easily in all things. Such an inner, experiential knowledge of Christ's love for us that surpasses all human understanding (Eph 3:19) comes to us through Christ as risen and ascended into glory. We now have the perfect High-Priest and Intercessor who reveals to us the self-emptying love of God's uncreated energies, unfolding in each moment.

To Be Eucharist

It is in the Divine Liturgy that we Christians come into the Body of Christ, the Church, and there symbolically celebrate Christ's death, resurrection and His outpouring of His Spirit upon His disciples. As we receive the symbols of bread and wine, through the transformative power of the Holy Spirit, the symbols actually become for us the fullness of Jesus Christ.

He reveals and effects through His Spirit that, as He and the Father are one in the Spirit of love, so in the same Love we become *eucharist*, a gift of returned gratitude and a self-emptying love to God. But we are called to be our true selves by becoming what we have seen and touched and tasted and consumed. We are commissioned to discover who we are by going forth to be eucharist to all persons whom we meet. We are to become Christ!

Yet we are to become also our true selves in our union with Him and the Father through their Holy Spirit. The answer to the question that is the title of this book is the answer you and I must give now during our earthly journey and for all eternity by self-emptying, loving service to God and neighbor. This is the good news Jesus brings us. No other news can beat this.

Feast of Our Lady's Assumption   George A. Maloney, S.J.
August 15, 1986

Chapter One:

WHO DO YOU SAY YOU ARE?

Who do you say you are? There can be no true progress in your spiritual life unless you uncover the hidden areas within you. These areas often pre-determine your actions and re-actions, usually coming out of your genetic inheritance through your parents, in touch with your blood line of ancestors. Such pre-determinational factors come also out of your own personal consciousness, now predominantly lodged in your unconscious.

Are you ready to go deeper and cry out to Jesus Christ, the Divine Physician, for the healing of your false self and the emergence of your true self in conscious, loving relation with God's Word made flesh? Here I present a disciplined method for discovering your true, beautiful self in Christ.

Who Do You Say You Are?

Stand sometime before a mirror and look deeply at the person you see there. Do you really know who you are? Are you pleased with yourself? Let this inspection go deeply into your self-identity, beyond the externals that are reflected back to you: "Is my hair combed? Make-up too much or too little? Are those more wrinkles I see than last week?"

When you and I look beyond superficial externals, we see a composite image of one who has been created by ourselves, by our parents and by others.

All your waking life-time, you have been busy painting on the inner canvas of your mind, your self-image. That image contains many factors from your genetic pre-programming, inherited through your parents' genes, linking you to a long line of ancestors who extend themselves back to the first man and woman. Your parents, knowingly or unknowingly, have fashioned for you both negative and positive evaluations of yourself. Parts of your self-image have developed from the negative opinions projected upon you by your parents and/or siblings.

As a result of needs unfulfilled in early childhood, all of us have suffered what Dr. Arthur Janov terms "the primal pains." We ache in the depths of our conscious and unconscious to have these basic needs satisfied. But worse, such pains create tensions and a split, according to Dr. Janov, between our *real* self, the subject of these desired needs, and our *unreal* self.

The unreal self is created in defense, to avoid greater pain. In his book, *The Primal Scream*, Dr. Janov writes:

> The child is born into his parents' needs and begins struggling to fulfill them almost from the moment he is alive. He may be pushed to smile (to appear happy), to coo, to wave bye-bye, later to sit up and walk, still later to push himself so that his parents can have an advanced child. As he develops, the requirements upon him become more complex. He will have to get A's, to be helpful and do his chores, to be quiet and undemanding, not to talk too much, to say bright things, to be athletic. What he will not do is to be himself . . . Each time a child is not held when he needs to be, each time he is shushed, ridiculed, ignored, or pushed beyond his limits, more

weight will be added to his pool of hurts . . . As the assaults on the real system mount, they begin to crush the real person.

The Unreal Self

The unreal self begins to emerge as the one that receives less of the hurts. But this self begins to grow farther away from the real self, which becomes more and more suppressed into the unconscious. We struggle, then, to live according to our unreal self because such an approach to life is less painful. We forget what it feels like being spontaneous and free, because now we have lived so long with our false self that in our pained insecurity we fight to maintain that image of ourselves as our true "secured" self.

This explains how very fiercely aggressive we can be when our unreal self is temporarily unmasked by others. We treat those who often truly love us as though they were our great enemies. This is seen often in the hate-love ambivalence found among married couples.

How uncomfortable and defenseless we feel in the impotence of serious sickness, above all, before death, or even in times of a spiritual retreat away from our hibitual society, and hence roleplaying, when our real self begins to show its head with a promise of what could be. Still we return sooner or later to "normalcy" and feel much better that things are as they always were!

Self-Image of St. Paul

In 1 Cor 15:1-11, St. Paul gives us his self-image which he developed over years of self-searching in honest appraisal of his failures and his talents as seen in Jesus Christ. He tells us that he is the least of the apostles. He persecuted God's Church. He doesn't deserve to be called an apostle. And yet he can say, ". . . but by God's grace that is what I am, and the grace that he gave me has not been fruitless. On the contrary, I, or rather the grace of God that is with me, have worked harder than any of the others; but what matters is that I preach what they preach, and this is what you all believed" (1 Cor 15:10-11).

St. Paul had a balanced, right view of himself. He learned by being in touch with his ego-image that in the past he was a sinner. There was still a principle within him warring against his true self in Christ, seeking to destroy his virtuous self. There was "sin" in his members (Rm 7:23).

Yet in spite of his sinfulness and brokenness, the "sting in his flesh," (2 Cor 12:7) was the occasion for him, through the grace of Jesus Christ, to be able to do all things in Him who became St. Paul's true source of strength and virtue.

Discovering Your True Self

How can you enter into such a radical healing that goes so far beyond your little backaches and moods of depression, yet includes all of these? How can you build up your new and true self, and discover the person God has always seen you in potentiality to be in Christ Jesus? The first step is to be able to look at yourself on all levels of your brokenness. This means a sincere readiness to go beyond the level of controlled consciousness and to enter into the inner, *real* self which remains hidden under the many layers of "paint" that constitute what you habitually think yourself now to be.

You need a healthy disgust for yourself as the first stage of putting on the new creation in Christ (2 Cor 5:17). You need a nostalgia such as the Prodigal Son experienced as he fed the swine and pondered his separation from his loving father. Convinced that you are living in a predominantly unreal world, you then cry out for a real healing reconciliation between yourself and God, with your neighbor and the whole material world around you. "I will leave this place and go to my father and say: Father, I have sinned against heaven and against you; I no longer deserve to be called your son" (Lk 15:18).

True repentance brings tears that pour out, like soft rain falling on the hard earth to soften it. The shell around your false world splits and God's penetrating love filters into your heart to stir into new life the great potential lying there.

Such healing must be an on-going process of continually meeting God's love in prayerful communion. What has developed over so many years of self-centered living, as though the world revolved around yourself, cannot be healed in one moment. It will come about only through God's love, His uncreated energies touching you and calling you into an intimate relationship in love with Jesus Christ. The Spirit reveals how much God the Father truly loves you (Jn 16:27) through the infinite love of Jesus dying for love of you.

The Inner Search

To enter into your inner being, you must embrace silence. This is more than a mere refraining from speaking. It is an inward movement into what Scripture calls the "heart" of man. It is going beyond the controlled knowledge you entertain of yourself and the world around you. How we all resist this silencing of our own urge to create a world based on our selfish projections! We will do almost anything to remain "up" on top, in command of our lives by means of our intellectual powers. In any situation, you have the power to fashion it by your mind according to your liking. You can truly create whatever world you want, depending on your psychic needs. And how mistakenly this is called "creative" power!

It is in reality your power for undoing yourself and putting off the whole process of becoming a healed, wholly integrated person, the one who corresponds to the name and person God knows you to be when from the depths of your being He calls you by your name (Is 43:1). We all are masters at avoiding a confrontation with the real person that we are in God's eyes. We play games, put on masks, become distracted by words and values that people around us live by. We can even busy ourselves "saying" prayers or talking busily to God, in a dialogue whose script we have written. Yet we refuse to look in real silence and poverty of spirit at our inner feelings, seeing both the light and the darkness that are struggling for possession of us. We fear to look inward with honesty, with purity of heart, to ask for healing from the Transcendent God when we see, through genuine self-knowledge, what needs to be sacrificed, what needs to be transformed.

Centering Prayer

Various words have been used by persons who practice and teach ways of making contact with one's deeper self. Transcendental Meditation is one description of a technique using Hindu meditation techniques made famous by Maharishi Mahesh Yogi (TM). Most of the Far Eastern religions, including Zen Buddhism, have similar meditation techniques. Silva Mind-Control and a host of other mind-expanding systems, along with hypnosis, use similar methods of breaking one's habitually controlled level of conscious brainwave activity to enter into a relaxed state, more totally in touch with one's deeper parts. Some Christian and Unitarian groups that favor developing the inner powers of the psyche through meditation use the term *metaphysical*.

For Eastern Christians, who inherited the *hesychastic* type of prayer from the Desert Fathers, a centering process is used that employs the Christian *mantra* of the Jesus Prayer. The "heart" is opened up to the healing power of the indwelling Trinity.

Whatever technique is used, we must always realize that it is in a faith vision that we wish to be centered, so as to receive God's loving energies, and, surrendering to them, we may find deep healing. This opening of the psyche, especially of layers of the unconscious, can be extremely dangerous. Instead of healing, we can release the demonic and fall into great fears and guilt. Repressed material that has been drowned in the unconscious can rear threateningly to disturb one in prayer. Sexual feeling can arise, influencing the whole body. The strange faces of the demonic flash, now brilliantly, now darkly from within. The many fears, anxieties, moods of anger, depression and hatred that come upon us from no apparent outside cause are indications of a smoldering volcano lying deep beneath the surface of our habitual knowledge of self. This is precisely why we need a strong faith vision of God's loving presence. We can then consciously place all such disturbances under His healing love.

Moving Into Inner Healing

As your spirit moves into a harmony with God's Spirit, you feel great loving energies uniting you with God, with your neighbor and the entire world. The walls of defensiveness that you have built up, the aggressive moods of attack to preserve your false identity, dissolve before God's love and your new-found sense of oneness with all the universe. You feel yourself entering into a new integration of spirit, soul and body. By such daily prayer you can release great powers of inner healing that will flow over your psyche and even your body, bringing healing and new strength.

As you yield to the indwelling Trinity and allow yourself to be loved, you experience a movement into a new freedom as a child of God, who loves you infinitely in Christ Jesus through His Spirit.

Your potential for *being* expands into a realized consciousness. You are being healed! The inner transformation that St. Paul speaks of (Eph 4:23-24) is experienced by you as now taking place within you. Unsuspected powers to love, to be towards God in total surrendering oblation, towards yourself in a healthy self-love, towards others, open up slowly. How exciting to feel the healing power of God's love dissolve the tight bonds of enslavement from so much of the past, from so much that you never even realized could have been a source of non-life in you.

Your Healing

Today you hear very much in Christian circles about healing. Faith healers are seen in huge healing services across the land via television. Huge rallies feature faith healers similar to Oral Roberts and the late Kathryn Kuhlman. The charismatic renewal has enlivened the faith of many Christians, including Catholics, to believe that Jesus Christ still walks this earth and does heal the broken ones, as He did during His public ministry.

You probably have experienced such healings in a prayer group, or in a special healing of memories service as you are led back into your past. As you surrendered the suppressed pains and hurts and unforgiveness to Jesus, you experienced inner healing and a movement toward wholeness. You have undoubtedly experienced healings through your reception of the sacraments, especially the Rite of Reconciliation and above all the Eucharist. Keeping a journal, through which you can dialogue with your inner psyche, could perhaps be an occasion for exposing unhealed areas of your past to the healing touch of Christ.

Evening Reflection

There are many ways to make contact with the elements that make up your false self in order that the real self with God's grace may come forth. I would like to propose to you an ongoing method of submitting your falsity, your brokenness of each day to the healing power of the Lord, especially to be done in the evening before retiring. God has spoken His Word to you in so many diverse and enriching ways throughout your day. Spend fifteen minutes reflecting in a prayerful manner upon those portions of your day. I deem it vitally necessary for all serious Christians desirous of making progress in the spiritual life that at least the last thing you do before falling off to sleep is to turn prayerfully to God in a transcendent reflection upon the day's events.

You spend about one-third of your existence in sleep. Much happens during that time of sleep. It is most important to put the events of the day into order before going to sleep. Your unconscious is like a huge closet capable of receiving an unlimited amount of sense experiences. As long as you are conscious during your waking hours much material is being fed into the unconscious through your senses. If this material is not brought into meaningfulness in terms of ultimate orientation, it tends to build up psychic tensions and anxieties. You cannot live long without direction and meaning that transcends your basic and immediate needs. You have been made by God for greater transcendent meaning than what you can ever grasp at any given moment.

You also know from your own experience that if you go to sleep with anxieties, fears, hatred, these things continue to prey on your unconscious, building up greater anxieties, creating a greater false self. We know also that what we last thought of in the evening is usually the first thing that we begin to think about upon awakening from sleep. If your nightly thoughts were centered in peace and joy and love upon God, with all fears of the day banished through childlike trust in His forgiving mercy, your sleep would be most refreshing and upon arising, you would find your thoughts drawn toward the transcendent. This focus on God's loving presence can continue throughout the day with your cooperation. Fearful thoughts while falling asleep give rise to fearful thoughts on arising, and an existential *angst* or fear might well continue to multiply throughout the day in a scattered diffusion of your forces.

How to Do It

We are usually drawn to exciting methods that border on the exotic. This is, however, a simple ancient method, found throughout the entire Christian history of spirituality. You will see the effects, if you stay with it, to create a "true" image of yourself as God would see you in Christ.

PREPARATION: Each evening before retiring, place yourself in the presence of God. Recall by an act of faith, adoration, hope and love that God is present, Father, Son and Holy Spirit. In their holy presence you wish to listen to the many ways in which God has loved you this day. You wish to be accountable for His graces, so you are eager to see how you responded. Honesty and sincerity are essential.

THANKSGIVING: Begin by prayerfully thanking God for the many gifts He has given you in the past day. Thank Him always in detail as you sensitively recall the many wonderful ways He gave Himself to you in so many gifts. Thank Him for the great, general gifts that always are with you. Then in particular for the special gifts of that day. Praise God for the food, drink, sleep, recreation, moments of happiness, your work of the day. Push yourself in faith to thank Him for having been present and loving in those moments of trial and the cross. Believe that all things work unto good (Rom 8:28).

PETITION: Ask the Father and Jesus to release their Holy Spirit to enlighten you to trace through this day and discover the many ways God spoke His existential word in continuity with His prophetic word in Scripture. Move humbly into God's perspective and judgment of things. This is the essence of transcendent self-presence to God's self-presence to you.

REVIEW: Go through the day moment by moment, event by event, person by person as they passed through your day. Observe how you responded in your true or false self to God's Word. Thank Him for the loving responses. See where you failed, hurt someone out of your false self. Get in touch with the moods and feelings that seemingly pre-programmed your words, actions or even omissions.

HEALING SORROW: The main emphasis of this entire exercise should be on asking God to forgive, to heal you of any failings, injuries, hurts on the physical, psychic and spiritual levels. Ask Him to heal those whom you may have offended or hurt that day. Cry out for the healing power of the compassionate Lord Jesus. "Lord Jesus Christ, Son of God, have mercy on me, a sinner." See Jesus placing His healing hands upon you. See yourself being healed in this or that relationship or hurt. Bathe yourself in the new strength that comes to you through God's forgiving love.

SURRENDER: Abandon to the loving energies of God the forthcoming day of tomorrow. See briefly the day without much anxiety or planning. Simply offer it to God. Beg Him to bless it and be there in your consciousness in each moment with His loving care, so that it may be the "best" day of your life. Then go to sleep in peace.

Tagore, the Hindu poet, wrote:

> I slept and dreamt that life was joy.
> I awoke and saw that life was duty.
> I acted and behold duty was joy.

Through such a simple exercise, faithfully performed each evening, you will be able to shed the ill-fitting skin of your false self and discover the true you that the Father has always seen you to be in Christ Jesus.

Chapter Two:

OBEDIENCE, LOVE AND FREEDOM

We Christians have received so much in and through Jesus Christ. But does such richness and insight into God's very own trinitarian family transform our lives radically? It seems to me the reason why we do not actuate in our lives and around us in our world the treasures of our Christian faith is that we do not sufficiently experience, person-to-person, God's self-emptying love.

If we daily encountered God's passionate all-consuming love for us individually, our response would be similar to that of Jesus. Overwhelmed in His earthly journey by the out-pouring of the Father's gift of Himself through the Holy Spirit, Jesus accepted the call of the Father by *obedience*. He obeyed the Father in a joyful delight and not in any fear because Jesus experienced the power and the gentleness, the richness and the self-emptying love of the Father for Him. He was able to overcome any temptation toward self-centeredness by acting *freely* in returning Himself as a loving response in obedience to the Father in all things.

As we prepare for a fuller share in the resurrection of Jesus Christ, let us reflect upon our level of obedience to respond to God's Word of love spoken to us in each moment. We will be able to measure the degree of our returned love and how free we really have become through our real experience of God's infinite love.

Obedience, Love and Freedom

How great is God's love for us! St. Paul links the manifestation of God's passionate, out-poured, self-emptying love for each of us with the obedience of Jesus, through His self-emptying, kenotic love, when He became obedient unto death, "even to accepting death, death on a cross" (Ph 2:6-8). Now we know what God is like. He is like the Suffering Servant, Jesus. God truly loves us and seeks to live, not for His own purpose but for our happiness. He has died for love of us!

How do we respond to such a divine, "passionate" love which God pours into our hearts, especially in those precious moments when we are alone with the Alone? Let us examine in detail the essence of Christian obedience to God's loving call and make connections between obedience and freedom and love.

True Love Obeys

True love is always self-emptying in loving service toward the one we love. Obedience to Christ is the index of our love for Him and of our loving union with Him. While reading the early Fathers of the desert, I have often been impressed by the fact that the one work they assigned to all Christians, regardless of their state of life, is to observe in loving obedience the commands of Christ. But this is only because these athletes for Christ understood the true nature of love as self-surrender in obedience to Christ.

We hear from Christ Himself that, if a person truly loves Him, that person will keep His word "and my Father will love him, and we shall come to him and make our home with him" (Jn 14:23). Keeping Christ's word, for Christians, should be more than the observance of the Ten Commandments. It goes even beyond observing all that Jesus commanded in the New Testament teachings.

It comes down to a state of listening to the indwelling Christ, as He, through His Spirit, reveals to you the mind of the Father in each event. But listening must move to obedience, for only in self-surrender in order to please the one you love is true love discovered and actualized. The end of the Incarnation is precisely that God's divine life may be restored within your inner being by Jesus Christ entering within your spiritual faculties by the divine uncreated energies of love. You should desire hungrily to possess this inner presence of Jesus Christ as light in a more conscious, unifying way. You burn within yourself to hear His voice. But what transforms your life into a godly life, living in love for others in the unity of all things in Christ, is your passion to allow God's Word to be done in your life through your perfect submission in obedience to His will.

The Joy of Obeying God's Will

For you there should be no greater joy than to seek out and willingly do the will of the Heavenly Father in each event. The secret of a truly happy and successful life is gauged by your seeking, as Jesus always did in His earthly life, to please the Heavenly Father in all things, in every thought, word and deed. It is a basic human understanding that if you love someone, you will "die" to your own wishes and live to please the other. You will wait on the wishes of that person and consider it a joy and a privilege to "do" anything that would bring pleasure and happiness to that person.

Thus true love of God is not proved solely by words, no matter how much you may say, "Lord, Lord," but solely by deeds, by observing the will of God.

> If you keep my commandments
> you will remain in my love,
> just as I have kept my Father's commandments
> and remain in his love (Jn 15:10).

This is never a humiliating submission before a powerful austere God, but a filial surrender to a loving Father whose loving activities surround you from all sides at all times. Doing His will is the source of your greatest joy. Because God is supreme, and the sovereign cause of all that happens, it is justice that demands obedience to His will. All inanimate creatures and all plants and animals *must* obey God's will. Only we human beings can freely return the gift of our being. This is why we become who we have been destined to be by God's love. We reach our unique identity only in God's love when we respond to that love in a process of continued self-giving in love. But this self-giving and response to do the will of God admits of many degrees of generosity in obedience. Our response will depend not on how much God loves us, for His love is infinite, but rather on how much we become aware of His immense, personalized love for us, manifested through Jesus Christ in His Spirit.

Christian Obedience to God

Let us examine more in detail the meaning of our Christian obedience to God. Often from childhood experiences we have derived a sense of obedience connected with a limitation to our own human freedom. Obedience may seem to us a restraint upon our wishes.

Remember how your father or mother gave you some chores to do. This was a command to do something which usually you interpreted as meaning something distasteful to you, but also it put a roadblock before your own plans.

True obedience in the Christian sense must not be seen as a sign of lessening our human freedom, but rather as a true sign of freedom. We experience immediately and intimately God's free gift of Himself to us through Jesus and His Spirit. God has a constant affection for us (Jr 31:3) and a dynamic, loving action to bring about our complete happiness.

Another element essential to Christian obedience is that as God calls us out of His love, we are called to a *responsible* return of such a free love. The word *responsibility*, before such divine love contains the word *response.* It is God's call that we imitate God's love, as in Ephesians 5:2.

We are dealing with God as a triune community of love, and ourselves, made according to God's very own image and likeness. We are dealing with loving relationships between persons, God the Father, Son and Holy Spirit and ourselves. This must rule out any thought of our subjection to God as to a despot. We do not face Him as a power which we fear. We rule out of Christian obedience any depersonalization of ourselves that would "force" us to obey God without any human choice or right to resist or to dialogue with Him. Any such submission would suppress our judgment and human cooperation, and rule out our liberty to respond freely to God's loving invitation. Fear would coerce us rather than the allurements of God's gentle, attractive love.

The Concept of Obedience

The word *obedience* comes from the Latin verb *ob-audire*, which means to listen to a call. It implies a readiness and freedom to respond favorably to a call given in love. Thus we are encouraged by St. Paul always to discern what is from God's true Spirit. "And do not be thoughtless but recognise what is the will of the Lord . . . be filled with the Spirit" (Eph 5:18). It calls forth from us a free decision in response to God's infinite love and goodness.

Believing in God's perfect holiness and goodness, we can and should give an unconditional love because through faith we are *certain* of His rectitude. "I know in whom I trusted" (2 Tm 1:12). We see how Jesus pushed Himself to obey His Father's commands with no little sacrifice in His agony in the Garden of Gethsemani (Lk 22:42-44). Jesus' love for His Father prompted Him to want to give more. He was sensitive to His Father's loving presence and He desired to be a loving presence to His Father by wishing to make all free choices in order to please His Father.

Human Freedom

God respects our free will. In this we bear God's image and likeness. He has endowed us with such liberty in order that we may ourselves determine, by free choices, to give ourselves as gifts to God in return for His self-emptying gift to us. He does not want robots, pre-programmed to a given response. He wishes from us a response that is loving and free, spontaneous and full of praise, joy and thanksgiving. God says to us: "You are my son/daughter. I only want your heart, your response in action that flows from your spontaneous improvising of ways to return My love for you. Choose out of love and I am thrilled as any earthly mothers and fathers are when their children return love with love."

There can be no coercion on God's part toward us since with Him there is only love. "In love there can be no fear but fear is driven out by perfect love" (1 Jn 4:18). We are not infants responding to God's demands, but His sons and daughters acting out of freedom as we determine for ourselves to return God's gift of love. In St. Paul's letter to the Galatians we see freedom to respond always to God's Spirit of love as a sign of our maturity. It is an obedience full of dignity and trust, totally free of any slavish fear.

We are to become in St. Paul's words "faultless children of God" (Ph 2:15). As God loves us in self-emptying love, so we ought to respond and imitate God by loving all others, even if they consider themselves our enemies (Eph 4:31-5:2). To love others is to imitate God and to be like His family. This explains the condensation of all commandments into that of mutual love. To obey God is to live in love always toward God and neighbor. And that is the peak of human freedom.

Principle of Inner Dignity

The freeing power of the Holy Spirit consists primarily in an ongoing process of leading us out of the slavery of sin, death and the Law into true liberty as God's sons and daughters. As He reveals to us daily the resurrectional power of Jesus' presence living within us, allowing us to live each moment in Him and with Him, we learn to accept our true identity. Living in the present *now,* we can live in the unchangeable eternal *now* of God's love for us in Christ Jesus.

The Holy Spirit progressively effects our regeneration into children of God as we yield to His power in us. The Spirit has liberated us from the slavery of selfishness or sin (Rm 6:17). We have truly been reborn from "above," not merely by water but by the Holy Spirit (Jn 3:5). Yet the Good News is that our rebirth is always taking place at each moment as the Spirit pushes us to live according to our inner dignity of being in Christ, a part of His Body, His brothers and sisters, and all of us truly God's children.

Jesus, The Healer and Liberator

Jesus came to free us, the whole "man," body, soul and spirit, in all our relationships. He came to give us life that we might have it more abundantly (Jn 10:10). His love, which is an exact image of the love of the Father for His children, was poured over each person whom He met during His earthly life. He looked into their eyes and poured out an infinite healing love that, to those who believed and accepted that love, brought them into a new existence.

Jesus came to image the Father's love, not ony in each personal encounter with each individual person, but, above all, in His "hour" as He hung dying on the cross. In His final hour of *kenosis* Jesus spoke God's Word of total love for us. Emptied not only of all human dignity but of the very last drops of water and blood, Jesus by that act has entered into an eternal act of always *now* loving us with such passionate madness. We can at every moment experience a freeing from sin and loneliness, fear and anxiety as we reflect upon God's freeing Word.

Our daily life shows us the great need we have for the liberation that Jesus comes to bring us. With a little sincere reflection upon the way we perceive ourselves in relationship to God and to other human beings, we all too often see ourselves in insolation. Our *ego* tells us we are independent; we need no one else. Sin is the thinking and acting out of such a perception. It is a "bias toward self." I must take my life in hand and determine for myself my ultimate direction. My judgments about others are made in an attempt to keep alive such a belief that I need no one and I am really superior to all others. Ultimately, sin is slavery to illusions and the rejection of love. Sin rejects movement toward another in self-giving love.

In such a state we desperately seek to be loved by God and neighbor. Yet our self-absorption resorts to power and attack in order to retain the original perception of our independence from all others. Jesus comes as God's great love manifested to free us from the isolation into which sin has cast us. With St. Paul we confess that sin in our members has control over us. Wretches that we are, we can be saved only by God's power in Christ Jesus (Rm 7:24). Our strength is in Jesus Christ who alone can heal and save us from our false selves and lead us into the true persons we were meant to be in Him. "He is the sacrifice that takes our sins away, and not only ours, but the whole world's" (1 Jn 2:2).

Free To Love

Jesus' obedience to respond to the love of the Father that He experienced throughout His earthly life in each human encounter shows us the intimate relation of obedience to love and to freedom. Love is a free choice, as Jesus shows us, to give oneself to God and to others in a free deliberation. In the cross and death of Christ freedom is revealed as a gift. The Christian under the Spirit of Jesus understands that slavery to egoism is destroyed by Jesus' great personal love for each of us individually. And true freedom is now revealed as God's love in us bringing us into a slavery now to belong totally to Jesus Christ.

How beautifully St. Paul experienced, in his conversion, that true freedom which was total surrender to Jesus the Lord. Paul and other Christians are to pass from slavery to selfishness, sin, death, the law and the elements of this world that keep the entire cosmos held in bondage, into loving service to Jesus Christ (Ga 4:3). Paul, after his conversion, saw his freedom in being dead to sin and alive to God in Christ Jesus (Rm 6:10-11). Christ lived for him as the directing force within his life (Ga 2:20). He knew himself to be no longer a slave to a law but a son of God because of the Spirit of Jesus in his heart (Ga 4:6-7).

With St. Paul, all of us Christians share in Christ's own life, who now is risen and lives within us. Yet He must be further formed within us (Ga 4:19). This new freedom is one of service, of living, not only as Jesus lived, but living in union with Jesus so that He constantly can love all human beings in and through and with us. Christ's life within us, that begins as an embryo in Baptism, is to grow as we cooperate with Christ to live as free children of God, progressing "to come to unity in our faith and in our knowledge of the Son of God, until we become the perfect Man, fully mature with the fullness of Christ himself" (Ep 4:13).

Abandonment

Christ is to become more and more the center of all your thoughts and actions. Everything in you, the values that you choose to live and act by, must be brought under obedience to Christ Jesus (2 Co 10:5). You are to walk in a new life with Christ (Rm 6:4). As you learn to let go of your own control over yourself, over God and your neighbor, you find yourself progressively abandoning yourself to let God have complete freedom to do with you whatever He wishes. Your prayer becomes that of the obedience of the loving and abandoned Jesus in the Garden: "Not my will, but thine be done."

This is a movement of grace that admits of many degrees and manifestations. It is not a static relationship to God nor is it a passive, infantile surrendering of all activities and desires on your part, without exercising your responsibility to make free choices out of a loving self-gift. It is the unfolding of the infusion of the Holy Spirit's gifts of faith, hope and love. As you come to believe in God's infinite love for you, you learn to trust in His goodness in each event.

St. Therese of Lisieux describes for us in simple language what such loving abandonment meant for her:

> I have now no longer any desire except that of loving Jesus unto folly. Yes, it is love alone that attracts me. I no longer desire suffering nor death, and yet, I love both. I have desired them for a long time. I have had suffering and I have come close to dying . . . now, abandonment is my only guide. I can no longer ask ardently for anything except that God's will may be perfectly accomplished in my soul.

Abandonment is to live out your Christian Baptism by passing over through filial trust in God's infinite goodness from self-containment or self-possession to surrender yourself completely to God's will. St. Francis de Sales writes that it is a true death to whatever we may wish or desire in order to abandon ourselves totally to the good pleasure of Divine Providence.

This obedient abandonment, flowing from a progressive growth in love for God, is rooted in the unshakeable conviction that all things lie under God's power and that He wills only out of His nature that is *love*. God cannot will anything out of any motive less than His desire to share His goodness with us human beings. His will is always turned toward ultimate good and our own supreme happiness. If it is true, as St. Paul says, "What God wants is for you to be holy" (1 Th 4:3), then all that falls under His guiding providence ought to benefit us unto our eternal good and happiness.

Surrendering In Love Is Perfect Obedience

If the love of God within you begets love as your response to God, then abandonment is perfect obedience in the great movement of love toward the heavenly Father. Such a love contains all other virtues and is the fulfillment of the two great commands of God: we are to love God with our whole heart and love our neighbor as we love ourselves. Such love is a renunciation of all self-centeredness in order, out of love for God, to do what is perceived by the mind, enlightened by grace, to be the will of God. It is a total gift of yourself as you, in your human situations, seek to live according to the mind of God. Love is the key word in abandonment. But it is also the key to true human and divine freedom.

In such a convergence of obedience to God out of love freely given in response to God's perfect self-emptying love for you, you see how true obedience to God, true love for God and neighbor and true freedom are inter-related. God becomes truly your Center. Grounded in His stability, you enjoy peace and joy that no one can ever take from you. God rules you, not as a dominating tyrant, but as a Lover, who draws you through his emptying service on behalf of your complete happiness. You will not desire anything else (Ps 23).

Such is the result of living interiorly in the daily experience of God's infinite love for you. You live to serve God and, strangely, as you lose your life and abandon yourself totally to God's loving care, you discover your true self gradually emerging as a loving son or daughter of a loving Father, one with your Brother, Jesus Christ, and together you live passionately to glorify the Father. In this you experience greater love for God and neighbor but also greater freedom. You experience true freedom as the ability to take your life in hand in each choice confronting you and choose to determine yourself to become the person God wishes you to become.

St. Paul summarizes this entire teaching: "Now, however, you have been set free from sin, you have been made slaves of God, and you get a reward leading to your sanctification and ending in eternal life" (Rm 6:22).

Chapter Three:

ASCENSION

"Christ is risen from the dead, trampling down death by death and granting life to those in the tomb!" This is the triumphant shout of His victory over sin and death to be glorified by His Father as the "new Adam." Now He who was dead is alive and holds the keys of the kingdom of death (Rev 1:18). And now each year we, too, can hopefully celebrate our shared victory with Christ over sin and death in our lives.

Perhaps we can enter into the symbols of Christ's Resurrection and Ascension more deeply by going beyond the words and images used in Scripture and the Church's celebration of these two pivotal feasts. Resurrection and Ascension are two feasts that go together. Yet the Church stretches both feasts out over a period of weeks so we may contemplate and experience the meaning of what Christ's new life should mean to us.

He Ascended Into Heaven

Have you noticed how your understanding and participation in the great pivotal mysteries of our Christian faith, such as the death, resurrection and ascension of Christ and the outpouring of His Spirit in Pentecost have radically changed as your prayer has become more contemplative and less cerebral? As you learn to let go of the subject-object dialogue between yourself and God whom you envision as outside yourself, or "up in Heaven," you learn to enter more deeply into the mystery of God's intimate presence to you in a different experience of time and space. You move into this mystery of Christ's saving presence through symbols that open up a new manner of "touching" God, far differently from a rational, meditative way.

Your pictures of Christ in the tomb rising as His soul returns and enters into the dead body, yield to a new experience of Christ as dying, rising, ascending in glory to His Father's right hand, and impact your very life in a new and exciting way. These great salvific feasts of Christ become your celebrations also as you participate intimately in the commemorated mystery of Christ. You are rooted in your *chronos* or historical time; yet you touch the eternal *now* of God's time, His saving time of *kairos,* that the risen Lord Jesus makes possible to His followers.

The language of such feasts as Easter, Ascension and Pentecost, opens you up to the world of symbols, the key for you to enter into God's real world. Symbols are the signposts that lead you into communication with the hidden Trinity. They are "meta-rational" signs of an interior world that is very real, but whose existence will always remain closed to you unless you can learn to pray through religious symbols.

Carl G. Jung has pointed out that the impoverished West has lost the ability to live with myths and symbols, the archetypal models implanted in our unconscious whereby we can commune with the invisible world of the Transcendent Absolute. In a dehumanized, rationalistic world, we are rich in techniques, poor in intuitions. We are weak in "anima" (receptivity to the inner voice), but strong in "animus" (doing) in our prayer. Yet we are beginning to react to such a black-and-white understanding and experience of Christianity, and to long for a more immediate contact with the Divine. Many in the West are becoming interested in body integration and a wholistic spirituality, and exhibiting a growing hunger for deeper solitude and silence. They have found some helps in the practice of Yoga and Zen methods of transcendental meditation.

Others have become attracted to Eastern Christianity, so rich in ancient, religious symbols. Beautiful Byzantine icons, the use of the Jesus Prayer and the haunting Liturgies open Westerners to a deep experience of God as Trinity through vivid sense impressions, not the least of which flow from stirring religious music as liquid mantras that open up the individual consciousness and even the depths of the unconscious.

Liturgical Feasts As Symbols

One of God's choicest blessings bestowed upon me was my entrance, through priestly ordination in the Russian Byzantine Rite, into Byzantine Christianity. I celebrated the highly developed religious liturgical feasts that commemorate events or "happenings" recorded in Holy Scripture or expressed by the early teachers of the Church in dogmatic statements. Such teachings became "enfleshed" and expressed in beautiful, symbolic forms of liturgical worship. Celebrating Easter at midnight around the "tomb" of the Lord, erected in the center of the Byzantine church, was a "happening" now. And it was happening to us celebrating with Christ His historical resurrection. I was no longer a participator from the outside, as one reads about someone else's history. It was becoming my participated history also, as Jesus risen opened Himself to me and the celebrating community and allowed us to share in our resurrection in His new life, in His ascension, in His sending upon us His Spirit in Pentecost.

To express what I wish to convey, let us take the feast of the Ascension and "de-objectivize" the elements that for so long we have held to as having happened literally in our time and space or rather to Christ and to those who witnessed Him. This does not take away from the truth of the given feast; rather, it highlights the truth all the more, and through the symbols of language and liturgical celebrations we are able to share in the essence of the feast.

Our usual understanding of this feast is that Jesus stood on Mount Olivet ten days before Pentecost, and bade farewell to His Disciples for the last time. He literally lifted off the earth and rose up into the heavens. Yet He did promise to come back again in the same way the Disciples saw Him leaving. We usually look upon this scene with mixed emotions. There is something of the sadness that the Disciples and Mary experienced at "losing" Jesus. But there is also joy, because He promised to send them the Spirit, and that was why He had to leave. In that Spirit the followers of Christ would have all power given them. Thus we see Resurrection as the first in a series of liturgical feasts, each separated in their first historical happenings and therefore also in their celebration by a certain number of days.

If, however, we take the feast of the Ascension and link it up, as we find it linked both in the New Testament writings and in the belief of the early Church and in the early Eastern liturgies, we can understand how to use liturgical symbols in our deeper prayer to enter into a present experience of a powerful Christian mystery that brings to us tremendous applications for our daily lives.

Various Meanings To Ascension

When we study the scriptural accounts of the Ascension in the New Testament writings and in the liturgical celebration of this feast we discover two essential elements that are not contradictory. First, we find the biblical texts and these predominantly refer ascension to the *exaltation* of the risen Jesus Christ in all His humanity. But they also refer to the total Christ, the entire human race, including you and me, as exalted and lifted up into the inner life of the Trinity. This is our feast too! It should have great impact upon our daily lives if we can let go of the merely historical elements and become present to the meta-historical encounter of ourselves with the exalted Christ. This is an "invisible" reality that does not admit of historical verification by eye-witnesses.

There is also another element that we must consider and it is this that has almost exclusively preoccupied our prayer about the Ascension. It is tied intrinsically to the first element, but is of lesser importance. That is the description of a visible "ascent" of Jesus, apparently witnessed by His disciples. It is graphically described by St. Luke in his introduction to the Acts of the Apostles. His intent is clearly to speak in symbolical form of a definitive "leaving" of this earthly existence on the part of the risen Savior, in order to highlight a new and more important existence within this material world of ours.

This is how St. Luke describes the "ascent" of Jesus:

> As he said this he was lifted up while they looked on, and a cloud took him from their sight. They were still staring into the sky when suddenly two men in white were standing near them and they said, 'Why are you men from Galilee standing here looking into the sky? Jesus who has been taken up from you into heaven, will come back in the same way as you have seen him go there.' (Acts 1:9-11).

What is important in the Church's teaching about Christ's ascension is that He, the historical Jesus of Nazareth, son of Mary, who was crucified on the cross, died; this same person, totally human, also rose from the dead and at the same time was exalted by the Father into glory without any historical "earth-time" sequence. We could say (but even this would hint at something happening in our earth-time), that Jesus died on the cross, and immediately in meta-historical time, in timelessness of God's time, He entered into a new existence. His corruptible humanity was "exalted" and brought into the very life of the Trinity. Humanity was divinized. A part of our physical world is now and forever inserted into a new transformation to share in God's glory, in His trinitarian life.

This is what we should rejoice in. What happened to Christ, the God-Man, in His resurrection and ascension is opened to our sharing even now through His outpouring of the Holy Spirit. Something of this human existence has been penetrated by God's Spirit of love and so escapes the ravages of sin and death, and now the human existence, the "first to be born from the dead" (Col 1:18), can share His glory and exaltation with us.

A Now Resurrection And Ascension

Father Pierre Benoit, O.P., professor of New Testament at the Ecole Biblique in Jerusalem, gives us the essential teaching that the Church holds out to us through the symbolic images used to express this teaching in the accounts of the Resurrection and Ascension:

> The essential teaching of Scripture which is to be retained by our faith is that Christ through His Resurrection and Ascension departed from this present world, corrupted by sin and destined for destruction and he entered a new world where God reigns as master and here matter is transformed, penetrated and dominated by the Spirit. It is a world that is real with a physical reality, like Christ's body itself, and which therefore occupies a "place" but a world which exists as yet only as a promise or in its embryo, the single risen body of Christ, and which will be definitively constituted and revealed only at the end of time when a "new heaven" and a new earth are to appear.

What happened to Jesus in His resurrection and ascension could never have been witnessed by the Disciples in their historical time. It happened to Jesus, but in His new existence after His physical death separated Him from our historical time and space. That He came back by way of apparitions to instruct the disciples means that He came to them in visions, so real that they could touch Him, hear and see Him and thus no longer doubt that He had risen and was now one with His Father in glory.

In the theology of the Johannine literature, the writings of St. Paul, the Epistle to the Hebrews, and even in the gospels of Luke, Matthew and Mark, the ascension and the resurrection of Jesus form a unity. Jesus, in this early Christian kerygma or preaching about the historical Jesus to early converts, is raised from the dead by the Father and at the same time is exalted in full glory and is given full power to release God's Spirit upon His disciples.

The Gospel of St. John presents the crucifixion of Jesus as already an exaltation to glory: ". . . the Son of Man must be lifted up as Moses lifted up the serpent in the desert, so that everyone who believes may have eternal life in him" (Jn 3:14-15). Knowledge of such an "exaltation" or lifting up of the Son of Man cannot be attained to except through faith. It is a knowing given in faith by God (Jn 8:28). But St. John also shows the repercussion of the kingly exaltation of Jesus risen at the right hand of the Father in regard to the rest of this world: "And when I am lifted up from the earth, I shall draw all men to myself" (Jn 12:32).

St. Paul clearly teaches the unity of Christ's resurrection and exaltation. We receive the most primitive account of the bodily resurrection of Jesus in Paul's account of post-resurrectional appearances to the disciples (1 Cor 15:3-8). His point in stressing the witness accounts of Jesus' appearances to His disciples in bodily form is to accentuate the continuity of the historical Jesus with the "new Adam," the risen Lord of the universe. What has happened to Jesus, as a "first cell" of a new world, is in a way already happening to you and me and to the rest of the cosmos, only to be completed in the *parousia* or final recapitulation of all things in the power and glory of the risen Jesus.

Yet St. Paul's teaching is consistent in linking up the risen Jesus and His glorified, new existence with His ability to touch us through His Spirit and allow us to share even now in that same exaltation. Our bodies even now share in the glory of the risen Lord. This he clearly teaches in his Epistle to the Ephesians:

> But God loved us with so much love that he was generous with his mercy: when we were dead through our sins, he brought us to life with Christ — it is through grace that you have been saved. Both with and in Christ Jesus, he raised us up and gave us a place in the heavens.(Eph 2:4-6).

One cannot accept the fact of Jesus' resurrection without faith, built upon the witness of the disciples who saw Him in His bodily form. The same acceptance of Jesus' glorification in His ascension can be accepted by us only by a concomitant faith in His resurrection. Such a faith allows us to accept Jesus of Nazareth as the "Son of God in all his power through his resurrection from the dead" (Rm 1:4).

The same linking up of Jesus' resurrection with His immediate ascension to glory is found also in the resurrectional appearances of Jesus to His disciples. In the Gospels of Matthew, Mark and Luke, we find that Jesus is risen and in glory and then in human time and place He condescends to return to appear to His followers in human, bodily form. Resurrection and ascension take place together and so does our participation, even now, take place together.

A Powerful Intercessor And High Priest

Much of the language used to describe Christ's ascension is taken by the writers of the New Testament from cultic language of the Temple in Jerusalem. This is seen especially in the Letter to the Hebrews. Jesus is exalted in glory and thus reaches the fullness of His kingly ministry as eternal High-

Priest, interceding with the fullness of power on our behalf. Jesus ascends to the temple, the presence of God, to perform His priestly service and in doing this, namely, offering Himself as a sealing of the new covenant with His blood, He is exalted in power and glory. "But now Christ has come, as the high priest of all the blessings which were to come. He has passed through the greater, the more perfect tent, which is better than the one made by men's hands because it is not of this created order and he has entered the sanctuary once and for all . . . with his own blood, having won an eternal redemption for us" (Heb 9:11-12).

Ascension is our great feast, too, for it is God's declaration through the first Christian community that even now we, too, can share in Jesus' exaltation and glorification since we have now the most powerful intercessor standing in His humanity and divinity before the throne of the Heavenly Father, always offering His poured-out blood on our behalf. With Jesus who now intercedes for us before the Father, we are gathered up into a oneness in His power and glory. Even now we can be given "possession of an unshakeable kingdom" (Heb 12:28).

This feast has powerful repercussions for us as members of Christ's Church. Now His Body, the Church, is established in history in space and time, and already possesses a share in the priestly and kingly power of the risen and ascended Jesus. He stays with us, never leaves us, is our Head and we His members. He is now always pouring out the fullness of His Spirit upon His followers. He breathes His Spirit upon His Church members and makes Pentecost a daily event: "All authority in heaven and on earth has been given to me. Go, therefore, make disciples of all the nations . . . And know that I am with you always; yes, to the end of time" (Mt 28:19-20).

Christ's resurrection and ascension make our hope before a sinful, cruel world a light in darkness as we believe that all human history is now under the transparent and immanent presence of the gloriously risen and ascending Jesus Christ. He is in glory. He is interceding for us, His members, that we will also bring His glory to completion in this world. We are His ambassadors who reconcile this world to Him and to His Father, in union with His powerful intercession. There will be a final exaltation of Jesus united with the redeemed people and the world they have touched and harmonized into the plan of God through the shared power of the ascended Lord. ". . . you will see the Son of Man seated at the right hand of the Power and coming on the clouds of heaven" (Mt 26:64). Jesus will not come back in glory except by appearing in His members who even now "ascend" with Him in glory as they learn to live their death to selfishness and rise to a new life of love for God and neighbor.

Through this beautiful feast of the Ascension we have absolute certainty that Jesus has ascended to become the Lord of the universe and abides among us in His new, resurrectional presence, especially through our encounters with Him in the sacraments and in prayer.

Language and Mysterious Presence

Now we can summarize what has been hinted at earlier in this teaching. To express the mysteries of Christ's resurrection into a meta-historical existence that is beyond any scientific proof and known only through the Holy Spirit, the New Testament writers and the Church teachers have used anthropomorphic images that are tied to an ancient cosmology or view of the world, earth, the heavens, the angelic choirs standing above the earth etc. We need to recognize the limitations of such language and images. This necessitates our transcending the limiting elements in such spatial terms by remembering that such images have value only as symbolic carriers of worshipers into the true reality to be experienced in and through those symbols.

Can you still use such language as Jesus ascending into Heaven and sitting at the right hand of the Father? Such language is not to be strictly scientific and historical. It is effective communication insofar as the essential truth of the Ascension mystery is experienced, namely, that Jesus Christ has brought His humanity into a new existence that transcends the limitations of matter. He has entered into the "real" world of God and now has the power to share this with us so we too can "ascend" toward the heavenly realm.

St. Luke in *Acts* presents the Ascension in historical terms of an event witnessed in space and time by the disciples of Jesus. He wishes only to highlight the essential element of the Ascension, the invisible glorification of Jesus that can only be accepted by faith through the preaching of the Church. He saw fit to describe the last departure of Jesus from His disciples, which would leave the pilgrim Church, not without the ascended Jesus, but with a hope for His final appearance. Jesus left this earth to share His glory with us on earth through His Spirit, Who in the resurrection-ascension mystery can now be poured out in ever-increasing abundance.

Sharing in Christ's Ascension

When we move beyond the literalness of the time and space language of this feast as recorded in the New Testament, we can even now experience a sharing in Christ's Ascension. Here are some key points to be experienced daily that will make the Ascension our own feast-day as we stretch out to meet Christ in his Ascension.

1. The first truth of this feast is that Christ has been taken into the sphere of the Trinity, Father, Son and Holy Spirit. His humanity is forever one with the Trinity. Now we, too, can share in His power and glory.

2. He is now present to us through His Spirit. He intercedes through His High Priesthood of always offering Himself unto blood on our behalf. Now nothing is impossible to God and for us united with the mind of Christ by an inner revolution (Eph 4:17).

3. Now all our sins are taken away. We can by faith be absolutely certain that Jesus is now with the Father in His risen, glorified humanity, interceding on our behalf. Now the

Eucharist and Divine Liturgy are possible because through the mystery of the Ascension Jesus has entered into the Holy of Holies. Anything we now ask the Father in His name will be given us (Jn 15:7, 16).

4. Through this mystery of the Ascension Jesus is now more present to us, as He lives within us in power and glory through His Spirit in a new and more marvelous way than He lived on this earth. Now we have the power to live our Baptism of death-resurrection since we can experience daily the resurrection-ascension of Christ as glory and power in our lives. He who is within us is more powerful than any force outside (1 Jn 4:4).

5. Experiencing this mystery of the Ascension becomes the source of all our hope and loving service to re-create this world into a oneness in the body of Christ. His is our *Kyrios*, the Lord and Master of the entire universe. We are His hands and feet that bring His power to play upon this present world.

6. In a way Christ is not fully ascended into glory. As we live the mystery of our oneness with the risen and ascended Lord, we can become the "places" where the Heavenly Father is now raising us and the world with Christ to a new sharing in His glory. Resurrection and Ascension are now taking place!

Chapter Four:

GOD SPEAKS TO US IN DREAMS

As a child in grade school, did you ever look ahead and wonder what your life would be like down the road in ten or twenty years? And now you have lived through that time and another year of life is being given to you by God as a gift.

Surely the passing of one year can bring to our hearts some regrets. Perhaps we encountered our fair share of suffering for one year on the physical, psychic and spiritual levels. Some relationships brought special pain to us. Perhaps we caused pain to our loved ones, deliberately or inadvertently.

Still all of us might have hearts that swell up with humble gratitude to God for His many graces and gifts. We thank God for His protective and involved energies of love sustaining us in all trials.

Each year of your life lies before you as a rich potentiality. Much will depend on your choices in each event of each day as to whether treasure can be mined out of the potential locked within our body, soul and spirit faculties.

One of your richest assets for fulfillment as a dynamic human person living fully unto God's glory is locked within your unconscious. Over 95% of what you could become lies in the darkness of possibility. For this reason I have chosen the important topic of dreams as a way to open up your unconscious to God's grace.

God Speaks To Us In Dreams

God is love. And love is communicated in words and actions. God is a God, therefore, who is always energetically gifting us with the gift of Himself unto communion. He has created us according to His own image and likeness (Gn 1:26) in order that we might, through the power of our "soul" faculties of emotions, memory, imagination, intellect and will, receive His "speech" about Himself, about our true selves in relation to Him, about ourselves in relation to other human beings and the whole created cosmos around us.

Receiving God's Word admits of many levels on our part. To enter deeply into communication with God and listen with child-like obedience to His Word revealed to us is never a static act, but a continued process of greater and greater alertness, discernment and surrendering love on our part. It means hard work. It is the essence of what we call the "spiritual life." There are no easy ways, as the lives of the Saints show us.

The Holy Spirit, God's hidden energies of love, communicates and is self-gifting in order to accomplish mystical union between God and ourselves. The Spirit reveals or unveils God in many ways: indirectly, through the reflection of His perfections to be found in His creatures; through the Church, in its preaching and its mediating encounters with Christ through the sacraments; and through the teaching of the hierarchy. Many true communications of God to us are indirect.

Dreams: The Forgotten Language Of God

But God so loves us that He also communicates Himself to us in more direct and immediate ways. Such modes of revelation are in the area that lies beyond logical reasoning and sense experiences acquired from outside ourselves. One such "pre-logical" yet very traditional manner in which God continually reveals Himself, as we find in the consistent tradition of the Old and New Testaments and in the early Church until the 5th century, is the world of dreams and "waking dreams" or visions.

The prophet Joel prophesied:

> In the days to come it is the Lord who speaks —
> I will pour out my spirit on all mankind.
> Their sons and daughters shall prophesy,
> your young men shall see visions,
> your old men shall dream dreams
> (Ac 2:17:Jl 3:1-5).

Biblical and early Christian heritage assures us that God not only communicates to us indirectly but also directly through our human spiritual powers. There never was any doubt with people of the Old and New Testament that dreams and visions are forms of God's direct communication. Other forms are the gifts of prophesy, speaking in tongues and interpretation, words of wisdom, knowledge and understanding (1 Co 12:8-10).

Dreams And Visions In Scripture

Dreams and visions have equal authority as God's "place" where He communicates Himself in the Old and New Testament. Those skilled in their interpretation, such as Daniel and Joseph, were revered; those who understood the revelations of God to them, e.g. Abraham and Solomon, became great and wise. Those who were overcome by their inner experiences, such as St. Paul or Ezekiel, became great missionaries and prophets. Viewed from this perspective the entire Bible is the story of God's in-breaking into man's conscious mind through the unconscious.

Psychologically, we call a dream an experience we might have during sleep when we are unconscious. A dream is like an internal movie, a story that is being shown on the screen of our unconscious (even in technicolor!). This unfolds as a story in which we are involved as much as we are while watching a movie. Dreams involve us because through them, God communicates Himself, using images and symbols from our unconscious; He wishes to involve us in the contents revealed.

We see this on nearly every page of Holy Scripture. "Yahweh said, 'Listen now to my words: If any man among you is a prophet I make myself known to him in a vision, I speak to him in a dream'" (Nu 12:6) In Scripture God is seen as one revealing Himself in dreams and visions. God makes Himself present to chosen individuals through a messenger or "angel." St. Joseph, in his dilemma as to whether he should put away Mary after finding her pregnant, receives God's guidance through an angel in a dream. ". . . the angel of the Lord appeared to him in a dream. . ." (Mt 1:20).

The evangelist St. Luke records that Zechariah encountered the angel Gabriel in a vision (Lk 1:22). Mary also met the same angel Gabriel in the annunciation narrative (Lk 1:26-38). Yahweh appeared to Abraham in a vision, and in a dream made a covenant with Him (Gn 15: 1-21). In a dream Jacob saw a ladder with angels ascending and descending. God promised Jacob a vast multitude of descendants (Gn 28:10-19). Jacob wrestled with an angel (God) in a dream at night (Gn 32:26-29).

Moses had a vision of God in a burning bush (Ex 3:1-6). Samuel heard God speak to him at night in a dream (1 S 3:1-10). All the prophets received messages from God in visions and dreams. The entire book of Daniel shows us how God communicated messages through dreams and visions and gave to Daniel the gift of interpretation.

In the early Christian community God's Spirit guided the Apostles and individual followers through dreams and visions. When a crisis occurred as to whether Gentiles should have to submit to the Jewish laws of purification, St. Peter received God's guidance through a vision-dream on a rooftop in Jaffa (Ac 10:9-16). St. Paul continually encountered God in Jesus Christ in vision and dream from his first encounter on the road to Damascus (Ac 9:3-19) until the end of his life.

Patristic Period

During the first five centuries this same belief that God speaks to individuals in dreams and visions continued and was respected by the faithful and recognized in the nuanced teaching of such Fathers as Tertullian, Origen, St. Augustine, St. Basil, St. Gregory Nazianzus and a host of others. St. Basil and Evagrius, of the Egyptian desert of the 4th century, used dreams in spiritual direction to attain the hidden levels of the psyche, the unconscious, for healing the roots of human brokenness and for the release of powers and abilities to serve others in freedom and love.

The universal belief in and practice of encountering God's communication in dreams and visions fell into oblivion until the 20th century, when interest was rekindled through the great discoveries of the "layers" of the human psyche by modern psychologists. This restoration of dreams and visions as great aid to the spiritual life has come about also through a move away from "dry" Aristotelian scholastic theology toward a more prayerful reading of the Bible. The Charismatic Renewal has encouraged a recognition of God working in the unconscious as well as the conscious level of Christians in order to reveal Himself.

Can Your Dreams Heal You?

You might be asking yourself, "I know I dream, but I hardly ever remember my dreams. Then what am I to make of them when I do vaguely recall parts of them? I don't know how to interpret dreams."

First of all, let me assure you that you do dream, and every night. We spend one-third of each day/night in sleeping and in dreaming. If we sleep seven hours, one hour cumulatively will ordinarily be spent in dreaming.

From my own experience in dialoguing with my dreams, I would insist that we need to remain always in touch with this world of mystery. God does reveal Himself beyond mere sense knowledge in pre-logical, direct experiences that come out of our unconscious, that "gold mine" of potentiality waiting for release and actuation if we could learn to tap its richness in terms of self-knowledge and God's personal communication with us.

The second principle is that your dreams are always about yourself, at least about you in relationships with others. You are not a passive spectator. God is speaking to you. You are the subject, but you are also the observer of yourself.

A third principle is to avoid seeking a book, a person or God Himself to give you an "interpretation" of your dream. This reduces the mysterious communication of God to you to an "either/or" black-or-white situation. To receive humbly what God wishes to communicate to you, do not be concerned primarily with a static, pat interpretation, but rather seek to "actualize" your dreams by allowing the symbols to evolve slowly and reveal their truths to you.

You must become involved in an on-going, prayerful dialogue with God as you continue to amplify, re-enter and dialogue with your dreams, rather than settle for a one-shot interpretation that might miss entirely God's true communication to you. Stay in the mystery of God speaking to you in night and waking dreams and you will discover also how to pray Scripture on deeper levels beyond mere conceptual knowledge. Scripture will then become for you a two-edged sword, cleaving the soul from the spirit (Heb 4:12).

The Map Of The Human Psyche

According to Dr. Carl G. Jung, our human psyche is made up of the conscious and the unconscious. Take his example: imagine an iceberg with 4½ to 5% of its entirety floating above the ocean surface. That represents your conscious. In your consciousness resides your "persona", or masked self, that is an adaptively organized image of yourself – your way of meeting and coping with the world around you.

The remaining 95% that lies beneath the watery surface, Jung calls your unconscious. The unconscious is present and active long before the conscious develops out of the dark potentiality locked in the unconscious (between the ages of 6 and 10 years old). To increase the conscious out of the unconscious' potential requires attentive effort on your part. Your unconscious is made up of your personal experiences that have been stored there and forgotten, and also the "collective" unconscious. This, according to Jung, "is the source of the instinctual forces of the psyche and of the forms or categories that regulate them, namely the *archetypes.*" On this level, all human beings share a common heritage, i.e., basic unlearned knowledge similar to the instincts of animals. We tap into the unconscious mind of the entire human race, back to the first man and woman.

The collective unconscious is the archaic matrix of primordial images which go below and before any language. Here lies the myth-making faculty that is pre-logical and non-verbal. Here are found three universal archetypes: the *Shadow*, the *Anima* and the *Animus*. Our "archetypal" dreams that deal with the level of our integration as "whole" persons usually center around the appearance of symbols of the Shadow, Anima and Animus. The Shadow in our dreams is a figure of the same sex as the dreamer. The Anima is a feminine figure in the dreams of men and the Animus is a male figure or figures in the dreams of women.

The ego is the center of our consciousness: the person we habitually think we are. The goal of the healing and integration to which dreams lead us is the achievement of a kind of mid-point of personality, wherein the center of the total person no longer resides solely in the *ego*, but at a point midway between the conscious and the unconscious. This center is called the *self*.

A Dreamwork Methodology

To use your dreams properly in order to open deeper levels of your unconscious to healing and integration between the *ego* and the *self*, between the *anima* (feminine) and the *animus* (masculine), between the *rational* and the *pre-logical* or intuitive, we need a methodology, a way of going about studying our dreams. New ways that do not overly stress the interpretative approach, but deal primarily with the dream and all it can tell us are being developed through a Gestalt process and Jung's method of activating the imagination. The most helpful work I know of to develop such a methodology for working with your dreams is: the *Jungian-Senoi Dreamwork Manual* by Strephon Kaplan Williams (Berkeley, Ca.: Journey Press, 1985).

Briefly, let me present some questions you can ask yourself which may help you to work with your dreams in a deeper and more enriching way:

1. Do you really wish to remember your dreams and work with them? To help the recall of dreams, have always a pad and pencil at your bedside. Pray to God that this night He will instruct, admonish, heal and affirm you as He wishes.

2. Do you habitually take time in prayerful consideration after waking up to *re-enter* your dreams in order to *amplify* consciously the material that arose out of your unconscious through the dreams?

3. How is one to activate any given dream? Place yourself reverently and in a very relaxed attitude of body, soul and spirit in the presence of God. Pray for the guidance of the Holy Spirit. To *re-enter, amplify* and *dialogue* with your dreams here are some leading questions suggested as aids by Williams.
a. How am I, as dream ego, acting in this dream?
b. What symbols in this dream are important to me?
c. What are the various feelings in this dream?
d. What are the various actions in this dream?
e. What relation, if any, does this dream have to what is happening right now in my life? In my future? To something in me?
f. Who or what is the adversary in this dream?
g. What is the helping or healing force in this dream?
h. What is being wounded in this dream?
i. What is being healed in this dream?
j. What would I like to avoid in this dream?
k. What actions might this dream be suggesting I consider?
l. What does this dream want from me?
m. What questions does this dream ask of me?
n. What choices can I, and will I, make as a result of this dream?
o. Who or what is my companion?
p. Why have we not asked: What does this dream mean to me?
q. Why did I need this dream?
r. Why am I not dealing with this situation in this way?
s. Why am I not doing this in my life?
t. Why have I dreamed of 'so and so' now?
u. Where are my helpers and guides in life and in my dreams?
v. What is the difference between a 'why' and a 'what' question?
w. What can happen if I work actively with this dream?
x. What is being accepted in this dream?
y. What new questions come up from this dreamwork?

z. Will it be useful for me to make this dream a "waking dream" and amplify it further?

Allow me to conclude this teaching on dreams with a healing prayer that you can say before falling to sleep and hopefully enter then into your dreams, God's forgotten language.

"Jesus, through the power of the Holy Spirit, go back into my unconscious as I sleep. Every hurt that has ever been done to me – heal that hurt. Every hurt that I have ever caused to another person – heal that hurt. All the relationships that have been damaged in my whole life that I am not aware of – heal those relationships. Speak, Lord Jesus, this night and let me know through my dreams what You are asking of me, to have healed, to complement or compensate so that I may become more and more the unique person You are calling me to become by Your grace.

If there is anything, Lord that I have not integrated into a loving person, kindly reveal to me what is missing and what I should choose to do to correct what is lacking. Speak, Lord, Your servant wants to listen! Fill the empty spaces, the vast spaces of my unconscious with Your loving presence. Set me on fire with greater consciousness of how great is Your love for me so that I may be a giving-love to others whom I meet along the paths of my earthly life. Amen."

Chapter Five:

THE SPIRIT DWELLS WITHIN YOU

What a mystery and yet what a tremendous reality the Holy Spirit of Jesus is. And the good news is that this Spirit dwells within each of us, empowering us with His gifts to experience the love of God the Father and the Son living within us, and to live according to this dignity of being a child of God.

The first group of followers of Jesus was made up of ordinary men and women, much like us. They were weak and sinful. But they gathered in the Upper Chamber with Mary, the Mother of Jesus, and prayed expectantly for a new fire, a release of the Spirit. We all feel a great urgent need for this Spirit's power and guidance to transform us into true Christians.

The Spirit Dwells Within You

Once we lived in a world that we separated into two parts. Everything we saw on this earth was labeled animate or inanimate. Living things, such as human beings, birds, animals and plants all were "animated" by an inner soul or principle of life. Rocks and solid things like tables and chairs were static, "life-less," inanimate. They possessed no soul to give them an inner growing and directive force.

Today nuclear physicists speak much like mystics, as Einstein and his followers declare that nothing is static.

Albert Einstein, the great proponent of the theory of relativity, wrote this beautiful statement:

> The most beautiful and most profound emotion we can experience is the sensation of the mystical. It is the sower of all true science. He to whom this emotion is a stranger, who can no longer wonder and stand rapt in awe, is as good as dead. To know that what is impenetrable to us really exists, manifesting itself as the highest wisdom and the most radiant beauty which our dull faculties can comprehend only in their most primitive forms-this knowledge, this feeling is at the centre of true religiousness.

The Holy Spirit Unites The Universe

Our Christian faith assures us that God, as a trinitarian community of love, explodes in His *kenotic* or emptying love to create a world of seemingly infinite diversity. Yet all multiplicity is continually being guided by the loving over-shadowing Holy Spirit to fashion a oneness, the fullness of the Logos of God enfleshed in matter. The Spirit is moving throughout the material world lovingly to draw God's embryonic creation together into the definitive unity – the Body of Christ. St. Paul expressed the creative process as terminating in the cosmic Christ. "There is only Christ; he is everything and he is in everything" (Col 3:11).

St. Athanasius expresses such Christian optimism in a world moving toward an ordered beauty and harmony:

> Like a musician who has attuned his lyre, and by the artistic blending of low and high and medium tones produces a single melody, so the Wisdom of God, holding the universe like a lyre, adapting things heavenly to things earthly, and earthly things to heavenly, harmonizes them all, and leading them by His will, makes one world and one world-order in beauty and harmony.

Overshadowing of the Holy Spirit

From the Book of Genesis we see at the beginning of the creation by the Trinity, a community of an *I-Thou* in a *We-*community, the presence of the Holy Spirit as God's creative power. God's presence as loving "Orderer" and chief-Harmonizer is seen as His Spirit of love hovering over the chaos and the void like a mighty, cosmic bird. "Now the earth was a formless void, there was darkness over the deep, and God's spirit hovered over the water" (Gn 1:1-2).

God the Father utters His creative Word by calling His Spirit down upon the cosmos in a continuous cosmic *epiclesis* to "divinize" matter into spirit. God breathes His breath, His *ruah*, His Spirit, as the principle of life into all His creation. The beasts are sustained by His *ruah*. The heavens are also the work of God's breath, His Spirit (Gn 7:15).

In a special way God breathes His breath into man and he becomes a human person (*nephesh*), capable of communicating with God as one made to share in His very image and likeness (Gn 1:26). But man, by the in-breathing of God's Spirit, is called also to cooperate in harmonizing all of creation into a work of conscious love, a harmony of diversity in oneness through love (Gn 1:28-30).

A Love Covenant

If God's Spirit is operating throughout all of nature, fashioning man, woman and all other creatures in a mysterious awesome way, His Spirit is more powerfully operating in His merciful, *hesed* covenantal love for His chosen people. God's Spirit comes upon individuals and His entire people to restore them to new love relationships with Him. God is most Spirit when He is renewing His people by giving them "a new heart." God breathes His love. Repentance allows His people to open up to receive His breathing-in-Spirit of love to become quickened again, to share life-giving relationships with Yawheh:

> I shall give you a new heart, and put a new spirit in you; I shall remove the heart of stone from your bodies and give you a heart of flesh instead. I shall put my spirit in you, and make you keep my laws and sincerely respect my observances. You will live in the land which I gave your ancestors. You shall be my people and I will be your God (Ez 36:26-28).

We have been made for communion, a "union with" God and fellow human beings. Another way of putting it is to describe God as love and we, through His abiding, loving presence dwelling within us and within each event of every day, are to receive His loving energies and thus live in communion through His Spirit of love with all persons we meet. We begin to move toward loving communion by means of "communication."

But communication is only the first step in becoming "present" to another. In language we relay information to another on a linear level. This information tends to be logical—facts, ideas that are comprehensible to our human reasoning. Our sciences are examples of such communication. We go to school to receive knowledge of facts. Our lives depend upon such knowledge. We also learn certain facts about

God given to us through His revelation in Scripture and in oral traditions.

But there is a higher level of knowledge. This is communion between friends and lovers, between ourselves and our loving God. This communion is effected through the operations of the Holy Spirit.

> The hidden wisdom of God which we teach in our mysteries is the wisdom that God predestined to be for our glory before the ages began . . . These are the very things that God has revealed to us through the Spirit, for the Spirit reaches the depths of everything, even the depths of God . . . Now instead of the spirit of the world, we have received the Spirit that comes from God, to teach us to understand the gifts that he has given us . . . (1 Co 2:7-13).

A Presence of Love

God becomes present to us and invites us into intimate union with Him through His Spirit of love. It is only God's Love, His Spirit, that can bring about true communion in love. When God created woman and gave her to man, He breathed His Spirit of intimate love into them and bound them together into a union, bone from his bone, and flesh from his flesh (Gn 2:23). God joined them together in love and they became "one body" (Gn 2:24) and no force in the world was to cut this union asunder. Christianity would guarantee that whenever we live in love toward each other, it is the Holy Spirit who is "perfecting" the love of God on earth (1 Jn 4:12).

In loving another, we become a gifted presence of God's Spirit of love to that person. We wish to live in union (the true meaning of "communion") with that person so as to be present as often as possible, not only physically in space and time, but more importantly in the inner recesses of our consciousness. We become present to each other in deeper and deeper consciousness to the degree that we can share our most intimate thoughts through speech. An often repeated "I love you," is not giving new, logical information, but it is moving toward deeper communion. We need words as the most ordinary way of communicating our inner self as gift to the other. Without internal words that can be expressed in externalized words, spoken or written or acted out in gestures, we would never grow in love.

But we human beings are this way because God is this way in His nature as Love. God the Father, in absolute silence, in a communication of love impossible for us human beings to understand, speaks His one eternal Word through His Spirit of Love. In that one Word, the Father is perfectly present, totally self-giving to His Son. "In him lives the fullness of divinity" (Col 2:9).

But in His Spirit, the Father also hears His Word come back to Him in a perfect, eternal "yes" of total surrendering Love that is again the Holy Spirit. The Trinity is a reciprocal community of a movement of the Spirit of Love between Father and Son through the Holy Spirit. God becomes real as He communicates in Love with His Word. His Word gives Him His identity as Father. But that means eternal self-giving to the Other, His Word in Love, the Holy Spirit.

The Word Reveals the Spirit of Love

From the revealed word of God in the Old and New Testaments and in the living tradition of the Church through the centuries, the Divine Nature is considered as inaccessible, uncommunicable to us. This is the awesome, transcendent God of majesty appearing to Moses at the burning bush; the God of Isaiah's vision who receives the constant praise of the Trisagion from the six-winged Seraphim who cover their faces with their wings out of reverence.

Yet Jesus Christ promises us that this inaccessible God with the life of the Trinity will descend and enter into our very beings. "If anyone loves me he will keep my word and my Father will love him, and we shall come to him and make our home with him" (Jn 14:23). Jesus Christ is the Word and the Son of the Father. He is the way, the truth and the life that brings us into the awesome mystery of the Trinity as a communion in its own life. All other names applied to the Word and the Son, such as Image, Wisdom, Light and Life etc. are summarized in these two central names.

Through the Holy Spirit we can believe from revelation that the Father begets eternally His only begotten Son through His Spirit of love. He gives Him His very substance, not partially as in human generation, but His total being, all except His very Fatherhood. Since the Son is one in substance with the Father, He, through the Incarnation, can bring us, not only to a knowledge of the Father, but He can actualize us through His Holy Spirit to be children of God, sharing in His very own nature (2 Peter 1:4). St. Athanasius, quoting St. Irenaeus, could summarize the end of the Incarnation: "For He was made man that we might be made God."

We Really Are Children of God

The Spirit that the risen Jesus sends by asking His Father is seen as the loving force of God Himself, divinizing all who are open to receive His Gift. This holiness given to us to transform us into heirs of God, true children of God (Rm 8:15), is the very indwelling of God's Spirit taking possession of us Christians, penetrating our minds, our thoughts, all our actions with the very life of God.

St. John, the Beloved Disciple of Jesus, cannot get over the miracle of our regeneration, ". . . not by water alone but by the Spirit . . ." (Jn 3:3, 5). "Think of the love that the Father has lavished on us, by letting us be called God's children; and that is what we are" (1 Jn 3:1). St. Paul never ceases to describe the main work of the Spirit as bringing us into a new life, a life in Jesus which regenerates us into true Children of God: ". . . the Spirit of God has made his home in you . . . . and if the Spirit of him who raised Jesus from the dead is living in you, then he who raised Jesus from the dead will give life to your own mortal bodies through his Spirit living in you: (Rm 8:9, 11).

Such a loving presence, so immediately experienced as an indwelling love, fills us with a new inner dignity touching all human relationships of body, soul and spirit. "Your body, you know, is the temple of the Holy Spirit, who is in you since you received him from God. You are not your own property; you have been bought and paid for. That is why you should use your body for the glory of God" (1 Co 6:19-20).

How can you and I ever again be lonely in the experience of the indwelling Spirit who witnesses within us by His gifts of faith, hope and love that the Trinity dwells literally with us and loves us with an infinite love? We possess the fullness of the triune God living and acting in love within us at all times, twenty-four hours of our waking and sleeping day and night. God cannot come to us in any fuller way than He, the community of love of Father, Son and Holy Spirit, is already living within us. The Spirit brings this new life to its fullness in the proportion that we allow the Spirit to become normative in guiding us Christians to make choices according to the mind of Christ.

A New Freedom

St. Paul was aware of the freeing power of the Holy Spirit as an ongoing process of leading us out of slavery from sin and death and the Law into true liberty as children of God. "Now this Lord is the Spirit, and where the Spirit of the Lord is, there is freedom" (2 Co 3:18). St. Paul uses the word "Spirit" to apply to the divine power, the Holy Spirit, sent by God through the merits of Christ and His intercession to effect the work of our sanctification, or *christification*.

He assigns to the Holy Spirit the character, initiative and salvific action proper to a person. Through his personal experience "in the Spirit," he had discovered the world of the Spirit. It was for him a "new sphere of life" (Rm 6:4). The work of the Spirit is to create this new life of Christ in us Christians. As we become alive by the Spirit so St. Paul exhorts us, then we must walk by the Spirit (Ga 5:16, 26). Christians are *pneumatikoi*, spiritualized by the Spirit, since the primary function of the Spirit is to create this life in Christ. St. Paul sees the world as tied together in the hope of being set free from its slavery to decadence, "to enjoy the same freedom and glory as the children of God" (Rm 8:20-21). We do not possess the fullness of the Spirit but we have come into the "first-fruits of the Spirit" (Rm 8:23). Still we have the pledge and guarantee of its completion (2 Co 1:22; Ep 1:14). Thus we can see that for St. Paul, the phrases "in the Spirit" and "in Christ" complement one another.

Guided by the Spirit

You and I are caught between two forces: the power of evil and the Spirit of Christ, between the unspiritual in us and the spiritual. We are to live according to the Spirit, the new principle of Christlike operations within us. The Spirit has created this new life of Christ living within us. We are now to be "spiritual", by turning always within to be guided by the Spirit. No longer is there an extrinsic code of morality, a Judaic Law or any other law operating. St. Paul puts it this way:

> If you are guided by the Spirit you will be in no danger of yielding to self-indulgence, since self-indulgence is the opposite of the Spirit, the Spirit is totally against such a thing . . If you are led by the

Spirit, no law can touch you . . . What the Spirit brings is very different: love, joy, peace, patience, kindness, goodness, trustfulness, gentleness and self-control. There can be no law against things like that, of course. You cannot belong to Christ Jesus unless you crucify all self-indulgent passions and desires. Since the Spirit is our life, let us be directed by the Spirit (Ga 5:16-25).

Only the Spirit of the risen Christ can bring us into true freedom. This highest, human freedom is self-determination in the inmost depths of our being. It is opposed to every kind of external determination which is a force or compulsion from without or from within. We enter into true self-determination only when, in the depths of our being, we touch God's Spirit, who releases our spirit to become a loving movement in freedom toward others. True self-determination and self-giving love to others become synonymous and are the freeing work of the Holy Spirit. For the fruit of the Spirit is love (Ga 5:22).

The basis of all true love for both God and other human beings is always the love of God which is poured out into our hearts by the Holy Spirit (Rm 5:5). We can consider the Holy Spirit as the applied love of the crucified Jesus, now risen and living within us. In prayer, the Spirit comes to our spirit and bears united witness that we are truly loved as the Father loves His eternal Son (Rm 8:15). God's very own dynamic current of love, between Father and Son, catches us up and regenerates us into new creatures, ever-more consciously aware of our inner dignity of being so privileged as to be loved infinitely by God. We carry the actual Love of God, the Holy Spirit in our hearts. This Love is operating at all times, even when we sleep. The Spirit dominates our spirit as we seek that inner revolution of our mind to yield to God's Word through the Spirit's love.

Listening to the Word Within Us

The Spirit gives us knowledge and discernment as to what God's Word is telling us from within us. No longer do we rely on our own powers to fulfill the command of Jesus, whereby we and others know we are His true disciples. Sin is put to death as we surrender ourselves to the indwelling Spirit. We replace ourselves as the center of reference with that of God's Spirit of love.

As we deeply experience the Spirit as the love of God for us in Christ Jesus, that same Spirit brings forth His fruit and gifts, so that we are turned outward toward others in love "because the love of Christ overwhelms us" (2 Co 5:14). Not only does the Spirit bring about a transformation in our consciousness that we are loved constantly by an infinitely loving God, but that same Holy Spirit is the loving energy that allows us to love others with His very own love.

Now we can do what sin in our members (Rm 7:23) prevented us from doing under our own power. We can fulfill the two commandments of God: to love God with our whole heart and to love our neighbor as ourselves.

We begin to live on a new level of being. We perceive ourselves in a new light. We walk in that inner dignity, all because of what Jesus Christ has done. "We are God's work of art, created in Christ Jesus to live the good life as from the beginning he had meant us to live it" (Ep 2:10).

We see the same world that we looked upon daily before, but now we see "inside." We see that all others are loved infinitely by God, even though they might not have experienced that same Spirit of love within themselves. We understand that we really are one with them. We "intuit" the Word of God, the *Logos*, in each person to discover that unique personhood in God's eternal creation of him/her in Christ, His Word. How can we now hurt anyone since all persons are our brothers and sisters, and we all belong to Christ's Body? How can we judge others who in their ignorance do not realize who they really are? How can we live by violence of any sort since we are listening gently to Christ's Spirit speak to us of how to live by God's loving energies in each circumstance?

The Spirit Unifies Prayer and Action

By contemplation given us by the Spirit, we can already "see" in ourselves the power of the Risen Lord working to transform us into a oneness with Christ and with the world around us. We can also see the power of the Lord Jesus working in the lives of all human persons, regardless of culture, religion, race or color. We are filled with Christian hope and optimism as the Spirit shows us the Risen Christ working in a constant process of evolving through the basic goodness in all beings made according to the image of God.

As we toil painstakingly over the little plot of this universe entrusted to us, we are buoyed up by the vision that this world was not conceived by God to be destroyed, but to be transfigured and brought into its fullness in and by the Spirit of the Risen Jesus. Freed by the Spirit from self-hate and insecurity, from all fears and anxieties, we can become the risen presence of Jesus in the world. Whatever we do, then, is done for God's glory, is prayer and action, transforming through the Holy Spirit the void and chaos into fullness and harmony of love.

Chapter Six:

LIVING THE MASS

In today's world we are challenged, as Vatican II's Pastoral Constitution on the Church in the Modern World tells us, to break through the dichotomy that separates our "sacred" relationships to God in prayer and our "profane" relationships to other human beings and to the entire material creation.

For this reason, the subject of this chapter is *living the Mass*. In the Mass the sacred and the secular converge as we believers fall down and adore the God-Man in matter. We are to become transformed, not from material beings to spiritual angels, but from self-centered persons into living cells in the Body of Christ. We are called outwardly to be co-sharers in Christ's High-Priesthood by rising above the raw stuff of our daily lives, over the sufferings and joys, the crimes and the conquests in science and are to claim all for the Body of Christ through our loving service. The Mass not only symbolizes the transformation of matter into Christ, but by our cooperation with the Trinity whom we touch in the Eucharist by touching Christ in all our daily work, sufferings and joys, we continue to celebrate the Mass by living it in every thought, word and deed. There can be no greater *true* devotion to the Sacred Heart of Jesus Christ.

Living The Mass

The greatest, most thrilling moment of my life is when I stand before the altar of the Lord to offer the sacrifice of Christ to the Heavenly Father through His Spirit on behalf of God's people. What humility comes over me as I am swept up into the high-priestly offering of Christ! Yet whether one is a priest, deacon or lay-person, we are all called to the infinite privilege of assisting, even daily, in this eternal drama of God's infinite love for us in His dying and victoriously-risen Son, Jesus Christ.

Yet do we really understand what the Mass is all about? Do we realize it is a symbol that actually effects what it symbolizes by giving us the power to live the sacrifice and the sacrament of the love of Christ in our daily lives? The Mass is the centering of the Trinity, meeting us in Christ Jesus in our time and space. It is the sacramental symbol of the goal of God's creation: a multiplied world unified by love, forming one Body of Christ in supreme worship and adoration of the Father through the Holy Spirit. Let us look at the Mass or Divine Liturgy and its riches in order to see how we can participate more fully in the greatest *action* on the face of the earth.

Christ Living In His Mystical Body

The Church is Christ continuing to live in His Mystical Body. The sacrifice and prayer of the Church are the sacrifice and prayer of Christ Himself. The word in Greek, "liturgy" is the name given to the act of taking part in the solemn, corporate worship of God by the priestly society of Christians, the Body of Christ.

As members of Christ, we share in His priesthood. We must, then, share also in His prayer and self-oblation. The Liturgy or Mass is a community action of the people of God in union with their Head, Christ. It is never the "priest's" Mass or "my" communion. All of us, priests, deacons, laity, with and through the one High-Priest, the Man-God, Jesus Christ, are called to enter into the common prayer of worship and adoration, petition, propitiation and thanksgiving.

St. John Chrysostom describes with joy and enthusiasm the part the laity play in the performance of the mysteries of salvation: "I mention and insist on these things to excite the vigilance of those who are in the lay state of life, that we may learn that we are all one body. We differ only as one member may differ from another; and, therefore, we should not cast all upon the priests, but should be concerned in the care of the whole Church as one common body." The Mass is a call to all to enter into the prayer and offering of Christ to His Father through the Holy Spirit. It is a call to enter into a faith vision that all Christians baptized in the Trinity belong to the Body of Christ. As a community, with Christ as its Head, all of us as members equally participate in offering and being offered as gift to God.

The Liturgy consists in sharing and is, therefore, the ground for community. The Greek Fathers call it a *synax*, a common action coming out of a joyous and solemn family gathering. The accent is not on individuals offering their own private prayers or silent meditation; it is on the total community, with each member realizing his/her privilege to be an active participant in offering and being offered with Christ.

We need to realize that in the Mass we take part in a living act. Every revelation of God's life and every episode of the life of the Incarnate Word becomes, in the Liturgy, a drama, an action, a reproduction and continuance in God's *kairos* or everlasting *now*. We are present and participating in the very time of the event of Christ's preaching, of His self-immolation on the cross, of His glorious resurrection and entrance into glory at the right hand of the Father.

God's Presence To Us

The Liturgy or Mass is both a source of theological learning and a form of vital action, for the worship of the Church is centered upon the self-revelation of God to mankind through the incarnation of the Son extended in time through sacramental prayer. God is present in three different ways. First, in Heaven where Christ reigns "at the right hand of God the Father," in His very human body, resurrected and glorious. This enthronement "at the right hand of God the Father, is explained in the ceremony of the consecration of a bishop: 'I say at the right hand of God the Father, not in a local sense, but in order to assert the external origin and glory which the Son possessed before His Incarnation, and retained unchanged after it. His holy humanity remains inseparable from Him and it will remain with Him forever. . . .' When we consider God as our Creator and Master, as Providence and Judge, we always refer to this presence which is our own presence in God and with God: 'Your life is hidden with Christ in God.'" (Constitution on the Liturgy).

God is present, secondly, in the Eucharist, for Christ is really and truly present under the species of bread and wine. This is an extension of His presence in Heaven. The gift of the Holy Spirit who is given through the death-resurrection of Christ is realized by and in the reception of the Holy Eucharist, which brings the human being, as creature, into a uniquely intimate relation with his/her Creator.

God is present, finally, in His Word, the Holy Scriptures of the Old and New Testament as God's inbreaking into mankind's history with His salvific self-giving love. St. John Chrysostom calls the Holy Scriptures: "a letter by our Heavenly Father transmitted by the sacred writers to the human race in its pilgrimage so far from its heavenly country. . ." The Scriptures are also a revelation of a rule of life leading us to our eternal destiny. Doctrine and life, thought and action, these are the two living elements stressed in our listening to the readings of Scripture, especially in the context of the Liturgy. The Scriptures are considered as another Incarnation of God the Word, or an extension of the one historical Incarnation when God gave us His only begotten Son. "For the Word of God is living and efficient" (Heb 4:12).

The Christian Passover

At the Last Supper Jesus gave the ancient sacrifice and sacred meal (the Jewish Passover) a new meaning. Referring to His cruel death on the cross, He says to us daily in the Liturgy: "From now on I am that Passover lamb, sacrificed to deliver you figuratively from the slavery in Egypt and actually from all evil surrounding your daily life. Do this as a memorial of Me." St. Paul writes: "Christ, our Passover, has been sacrificed" (1 Cor 5:7). Our Eucharistic celebration is a Jewish Passover with a new meaning. We celebrate this action of Christ as a *now* freeing moment by Christ of us from all enslavement, especially from sin and death that eat away from within us God's divine presence and life. This necessitates, therefore, our vital participation in a most prayerful, sincere way, that can never be finished with the end of the Mass. It is a call to live in that joyous freedom as children of God by embracing the cross of our own self-immolation to God in order to enter into the sign of true freedom, love for God and the love for all human beings.

How To Celebrate The Liturgy

We cannot truly celebrate the death and resurrection of Christ that are being commemorated in the Liturgy unless we move away from our own individualistic absorption to enter into the very mind of Christ as He is, not only in His presence at the Last Supper and on the cross, but also now in His eucharistic presence as He dies and rises into glory. "Do this as a remembrance of me" (Lk 22:19) is a command of Christ to recall what He did, what He always is doing in liturgical time, and to do this in His presence and power. The celebration of Mass is, therefore, the action of Christ and His people, each taking his/her appointed place and role in His Body, being of one heart and mind with Christ.

As the Liturgy is made up of two main parts, the Liturgy of the Word and the Liturgy of the Eucharist, so we are called to be instructed in His way of life, according to His revealed values, and then to put these values into action through the oneness experienced with Christ in His Father and Holy Spirit through Holy Communion.

1. First, preliminary to the Liturgy of the Word are the introductory rites of the Mass. This embraces the entrance antiphons, penitential rites, praise to Christ and opening prayers that set the theme of the Mass. Our attitude should be one of moving out of our darkness of self-absorption to enter into a oneness with Christ, so that when He speaks to us in the readings we will respond.

2. *Liturgy of the Word*. God speaks to us from the Old and New Testaments, through the Epistle, responsorial Psalm and the Gospel. The priest presents to us in his homily the call of God, through what has been heard to apply Christ's teaching to our daily lives. The profession of faith ties us to the apostolic communities of earlier times in our one faith, one body in Christ. In that oneness we join our petitions to the one intercession of Christ, the High-Priest, to pray for all human beings.

3. *The Liturgy of the Eucharist*. This brings, with the offering of the gifts of bread and wine, our own alms-giving for the poor. Here we see that the accent is not so much on what we are receiving in this vital part of the Mass, but what we are ready to give of ourselves. The Preface sings out the story of the Trinity's great love of mankind, especially manifested through the incarnation, death and resurrection of Jesus Christ. We are invited to enter into the most sacred moment of salvation history, on the night when Christ took bread and broke it and gave it to His disciples to eat, saying: "Take and eat, this is my Body . . . take and drink, this is my blood, unto the remission of sins. Do this in remembrance of me."

The recitation of the *Our Father* brings us into Christ's prayer, given to us as a way of life that makes us worthy if we live in proper loving relationships to God and neighbor to receive Himself as our own life, eternal life unto the remission of our sins. The receiving of Christ in the Eucharist is to empower us to go forth from the Eucharistic celebration to become a part of the Bread of Life to all whom we will be privileged to serve lovingly. The Mass is never ended; it only begins as a way of life when we leave the physical church to become the true Church, the Body of Christ, in our every human situation.

A Blessing To Others

In the Last Supper when Jesus first gave Himself to His Church-community as Eucharist, He gave a blessing. A blessing (in Hebrew, *berakah*) in the Old Testament was a creative act, whether given by God to His people or by one person to another.

In the Mass, you receive the Father's blessings as He blesses all living creatures, above all man and woman, and empowers them to be a similar creative blessing for all creatures given to man by God.

You receive Christ's blessing, His High-Priest prayer to the Heavenly Father, which empowers you to leave the Mass and become a blessing to others.

We do not receive the Eucharist in order to speak pious sentiments to Jesus, as an object of our adoration. In the Eucharist, we, too, like the first Disciples of Jesus, are swept up into the loving energies of the Trinity to become active love in service for one another and for His whole Body. Through the Eucharist, we break out in faith to put on the total mind of the Father, Son and Holy Spirit. In the microcosmic communion with the transfigured Bread and Wine, we are brought into a deeper faith to a cosmic communion, first with the Body of Christ, with those members living by faith in Jesus as Lord. There is no receiving the Body of Christ unless we receive the whole Church and this includes an openness on our part to love and serve the whole of humanity.

St. Paul tells us of the fruit of the Eucharist:

"Bear with one another charitably, in complete selflessness, gentleness and patience. Do all you can to preserve the unity of the Spirit by the peace that binds you together. There is one Body, one Spirit just as you were all called into one and the same hope when you were called." (Ep 4:2-3).

More specifically, St. Paul writes:

"The fact that there is only one loaf means that, though there are many of us, we form a single body, because we all have a share in this one loaf" (1 Cor 19:17).

Should anyone receive the Body and Blood of Jesus and offend in charity their neighbors, they do not recognize the Body of Christ by failing to recognize His members, and thus

". . . a person who eats and drinks without recognizing the Body is eating and drinking his own condemnation" (1 Cor 11:29).

Teilhard de Chardin beautifully describes this fruit of love that comes to us in the Eucharist.

The gift you ask of me for these brothers of mine — the only gift my heart can give them — is not the overflowing tenderness of those special, preferential loves which you implant in our lives as the most powerful created agent of our inward growth: it is something less tender but just as real and of even greater strength. Your will is that, with the help of your Eucharist, between me and my brother-men there should be revealed that basic attraction (already dimly felt in every love once it becomes strong) which mystically transforms the myriads of rational creatures into (as it were) a single monad in You, Christ Jesus (*Hymn of the Universe*).

A Eucharistic Presence To Others

The Eucharist is a sign, not only of our union with Jesus Christ and the Heavenly Father by the illumination of the Spirit of love, but, above all, of our union or our desire to work lovingly toward union with all mankind. But what precisely makes a Church-community a praying one? True community, according to Bernard Lonergan, is the "achievement of a common meaning." It is not fashioned by whim of circumstance nor does it arise simply from the accidents of geographical nearness. A true community is realized by a centration of wills in love, loyalty and faith upon a common vision.

The common ideal of a Church-community is its point of active convergence of individual human beings who, through faith in the indwelling presence of the Risen Jesus, under the impulse of the Holy Spirit, are on their way toward the Heavenly Father. It is an ideal that embraces all of humanity, eventually united around Christ.

In the Church, men and women are already being gathered together around Christ by the Spirit; and in the Church, the witness is already being given that salvation is now being realized. Members of such a Church-community seek to signify and to witness, both by *being* and by *doing*, that men are one in Christ Jesus. Such is the Christian ideal and how exacting it is! Only the force of God's Word and the power of the Spirit can blend our indocile hearts and wills into this oneness in Christ. In communion with Him, especially in a life of eucharistic communion, the community is grafted on to the Paschal mystery. Its weaknesses and sinfulness are entrusted to the strength of Jesus the Healer. The elements of death and division in it are transmuted into factors of life and unity. Love, the gift of the Spirit (Rm 5:5), transforms hearts and effects communion among them at the deep level of faith.

Energized by the oneness thus produced, love then issues forth into dynamic, apostolic service keyed to respond to contemporary needs. Thus, our dedication to these needs springs out of the heart of our community with one another, and our oneness with another is woven out of our involvement in a common purpose. What makes the Church-community unique over all other communities is the common faith, hope and love received in Baptism that allow each member to become incorporated into this community that is truly the very Body of the risen Lord Jesus.

A Cosmic Liturgy

It is almost a cliche to say that we live the way we pray, and we pray the way we live. The quality of our prayer-life is the test of the worth of the rest of our life. The quality of our real participation of the Mass, the death-resurrection of Jesus Christ, is measured by our going forth from the community-prayer to complete it in our living. Prayer, especially true worship and adoration of God, is perfect only in doing, in living according to the Father's salvific will. Prayer and the Eucharist can never be abstract or separated from our daily living. If it is true prayer, it must spring from our life and be expressed and completed in our life. St. Paul exhorts us:

". . . and worship him, I beg you, in a way that is worthy of thinking beings, by offering your living bodies as a holy sacrifice, truly pleasing to God" (Rm 12:1).

The problem of how to pray and how to live is really the same problem. It is the same problem of how to celebrate the Mass and how to build the Body of Christ. Personal holiness, rooted in your intimate communion with God, grows in your love's interpersonal relations for the love of God that need to be expressed in the love of the neighbor.

The Liturgy, carried out to perfection exteriorly, will be but a tinkling cymbal in the ears of God unless we who celebrate it continue to glory in the same Lord also in the economic, social, political and cultural fields. Our intense participation in community prayer and sharing in the Body of

Christ in the Eucharist are measured by the degree of our sharing ourselves with each other before the Father of us all.

Today, any serious Christian who prays deeply in the heart in his/her own personal, solitary prayer and in liturgical community is impelled to be concerned with the rampant poverty throughout the world. We cannot muffle our ears and block out the cries of our suffering brothers and sisters, wherever they may be in the world as victims of oppression, wars, natural calamities or psychological or spiritual deprivation. The important element in true, authentic prayer is that all of us will be constantly thrust forth into our immediate communities, and there we will witness to the Gospel values by fighting all obstacles that in any way impede the conditions for all human beings to grow and develop their talents in freedom and dignity.

For one who has recognized in the Liturgy Christ in bread and wine, such an act of faith continues as he/she sees on each human being the mark of the sacred blood of Jesus Christ, a part of Christ. For the Christian contemplative going forth from the Eucharist, there is no insignificant event that does not bear the stamp of the Holy Trinity's desire to redeem all creation and restore it through Christ to the original plan as conceived by that loving community of the Trinity. You share in Christ's high-priesthood power as you, in love, do all to transform the raw stuff of this world into His Body. This is not only to celebrate the Eucharist but above all to live it.

Chapter Seven:

FINDING GOD IN ALL THINGS

Modern Christians seem to separate prayer from their work, contemplation from action, vertical relations with God from horizontal relations with people and material creatures. Is it not true that you find it difficult to find God in all moments of your daily life? You find it easier to be in God's presence at Mass or in your prayer alone with God than at a party, or accepting insults from those around you. It truly is difficult to be present to God when you have to work so hard concentrating on your duties.

This is the goal of our prayer-life – to live so grounded in God's presence within us and around us that our activities not only do not take us away from God, but they actually become occasions for us to be constantly in prayer as we are present to Him in His creative co-working in love with us.

We are constantly invited by God to become with Him "co-creators" of this world, to bring it into a harmonious whole through loving unity of all God's creation in Christ. But we do not go from created things up to our Creator. Rather we always are to move from God, Trinity, Father, Son and Holy Spirit toward the created world. We discover by faith, hope and love God's immanent indwelling and "laboring" inside of each atom and we are to work in loving service with the triune God. It requires great discipline on our part to stand inwardly attentive to God's presence in matter. Prayer and work must go together. One cannot exist without the other. It takes us, however, most of our earthly pilgrimage to acquire facility in that which is the best preparation for Heaven which is a seeing all things in God and God in all things.

Finding God In All Things

You and I have lived most of our lives in a separation between our prayer and our activities. God's two main commandments seem to pull us in two directions at once. We have the vertical relationship to God in His command: "Love the Lord thy God with thy whole heart, thy whole soul, thy whole mind and thy whole strength" (Dt 6:7). This is a seeming call to desert, to silence, to interior prayer alone with God.

But, then, on the other hand, we are commanded by God to love our neighbor as we love ourselves (Lv 19:17). Do we not very often feel that our "horizontal" relationships with other human beings, when we truly love them, can pose a threat to our vertical relationships with God? How many priests, nuns and brothers have been trained to solve this paradox of the two commands of God by a loving, prayerful, self-surrendering of ourselves only to God? To other human beings we give service through our virtuous deeds. But were such religious and also other Christians taught that, when we love others, God's love for us is being perfected (1 Jn 4:12)?

Surely God would not command us to love Him and all other human beings with any anxiety or fear of the impossibility. The Saints bear witness that the more they were centered upon God as the core of their being, the more they were united in true, loving service to other human beings. St. Ignatius, the founder of the Society of Jesus (the Jesuits) teaches us, expecially in his *Spiritual Exercises*, that the Christian spiritual life is not a problem that opposes prayer to action. The spiritual life is fidelity to God which demands fidelity to prove love by loving deeds.

If we look at St. Ignatius' teaching, we can find a synthesis for our own lives. He based his doctrine on personal experience that came through meditating upon and living out the Gospels. In a cave at Manresa, Spain, at the beginning of his spiritual growth, for ten months he knew no other activity than continued prayer alone with God. He struggled against temptations and illusions, but he also experienced great joys and consolations. This left Ignatius with one desire: to live completely for God alone.

After consecrating Himself to God's glory and service, he went on pilgrimage to the Holy Land where he felt God wanted him to live close to the places blessed by the physical presence of Jesus while He was on earth. But he soon learned that God was leading him through his meditations on the Gospels to go forth in union with Christ, His Captain, His King, to bring others into God's Kingdom. This meant hard work and, above all, a lessening of his many hours of prayer alone with God. He returned to Spain and sat in school with children, learning Latin. St. Ignatius turned away from the consolations of his life of deep prayer to immerse himself in occupations of the mind in order that he might be ordained a priest and help people come to know God more intimately, love Him more ardently and follow Him in Christ Jesus more closely. He moved to busy, distracting Paris to study theology at the university for several more years.

We see a principle in his life. When he had no occupations at hand for God's greater glory, he gave more time to devotions, study of Scripture and to asceticism. But when he was involved in teaching and preaching Christian doctrine or with the important work of studying in order one day to help others know God, he shortened his time of formal prayer. He thought it to be more pleasing to God to give more time and efforts in loving services, undertaken for God's glory. Over eleven years of such study and labor, he developed a great interior liberty. He had shown himself faithful to human means in loving his Master, indifferent toward further spiritual consolations as opposed to what he saw clearly as unto God's greater glory to other human beings.

He achieved a spiritual liberty, a "purity of heart" that enabled him to see God everywhere, or, in his own words, to "find God in all things." Fidelity to do all work in union with God and unto His glory never took Ignatius away from God nor from prayer. This gives us his teaching of continual prayer in the midst of lives filled with great movement and action. He taught his fellow companions to find God in hard work performed in all areas of human life. The market place was not in opposition to the monastery or a hidden, contemplative life. God is everywhere; above all, He lives within each baptized Christian in a very dynamic, acting, loving way. God's creative love unfolds in the context of our human work as well as in aloneness with the Alone.

Mary and Martha

In the Gospel account of Mary and Martha, sisters of Lazarus whom Jesus loved, we see in the patristic tradition the reference to them as symbols or types of the contemplative and the active lives, the *anima* (diffused awareness) and the *animus* (focused consciousness) that must be integrated and not opposed in all human beings. Mary sat lovingly at the feet of Christ and listened to His words. Martha was busy in the kitchen, but apparently very anxious that her work in preparing the meal was taking her away from hearing Christ.

If Mary chose the better part, as Jesus said (Lk 10:42), it was because she was centered with complete attention upon Him to receive His words. Martha was preoccupied with herself and was "anxious and troubled about many things." She wanted to please the Lord, as all of us Christians wish, but she was focused upon herself and her desire, while Mary was totally turned toward Christ in loving attention.

This Gospel story should teach us that we are to give full attention to Christ who dwells within us. Then we busy "Marthas" will be able to work well and still not lose the "Mary" in us. We will seek to see God in all things. In our busy activities, conversations, in all that we see, hear, taste and think, we will seek to find the presence of God. His divine majesty is in all things by His power, His presence, His essence. We should not be surprised to find ourselves, in the early years of developing this more contemplative habit of finding God in all things, to be at times without devotion and to experience distractions, especially in performing our duties. If we bear these with patience and vigilantly check where we fail out of our false egos to remain close to our center where Christ dwells with His Father and Holy Spirit, we will gradually sharpen our faith so that we readily live in a constant "Divine Milieu."

Prayer, then, will become for us seeking God's holy presence in each moment and surrendering our deliberate wills to do His will in all things. Prayer is in this sense a spiritual attitude which finds God in the midst of even the most absorbing action. We will discover that in all our activities and mental concentration we can direct our spirit toward God so that everything becomes prayer. If we must interrupt our formal time of prayer alone with God to perform acts of charity toward others, we should hardly believe such acts of love are less pleasing to God than remaining in loving prayer focused exclusively upon God. "If we love one another, God abides in us and His love is perfected in us (1Jn 4:12).

Active Prayer

Little by little we should observe that there is little separation between what we do and the motive for which we do it. We will be one with God in all our activities through the same will-act that focuses us by faith, hope and love only upon God, even though we need to concentrate on the work at hand. Such an ability to live in the presence of God can be attained only by devotion to interior purification and humble fidelity to some disciplined time daily for formal prayer.

Faithful exercise of prayer at definite times is an indispensable condition for remaining united to God and for finding Him in all things during our busy activities. We will never discover God in the multiplicity of our daily life if we have not found Him in any concentrated time each day within ourselves. Yet we must not conceive formal prayer as a time of building up "spiritual capital," something we acquire in the morning and spend during the day, burning it up in a multitude of activities. Far from ruining the fruits of formal prayer, our activities must stir up new prayer, a deeper consciousness of God's immanent presence within us and within all of His creatures.

If we reluctantly leave prayer thinking that now we must leave God and go out where He is not, this will make impossible the devotion we need in all we undertake for the love of God. We return to prayer after a busy day of work that ought not to take us away from God's loving presence and creative activity to which we have joined our own free-willed creativity in love, to realize that our actions are at once the happiness and torment of love. We are happy at finding God in our work and in all human encounters. We experience torment at not being able to remain completely absorbed in God. There is a sort of violence that our love for God and God's love for us sends us into exterior works as a sort of a crucifixion. Our only desire is Christ and Him crucified, as St. Paul so often writes.

Love cannot be diminished in work undertaken for love of God and neighbor. But if we are not faithful to prayer, we must not think we can replace such loving surrender with action. Action, deprived of this necessary centering upon God in faith, hope and love through formal prayer, is scattered and lost among creatures of the world. All too often our hearts will be filled with self-centeredness. This is why Jesus says, "Where your treasure is, there will your heart be also" (Lk 12:34). Desire for prayer keeps us attentive to the needs of the Kingdom and the presence of God throughout all His material creation. We join His creativity to ours to work together in a synergy of mutual love.

Not Pantheism But Pan-en-theism

We are not asked to turn our mind away from what we are doing in order to make ourselves conscious of God's presence. Trying to divide our mind would soon become intolerable and the source of a thousand anxieties. We have only one thought process. We cannot at the same time concentrate with equal strength both upon God and upon persons whom we are encountering. But unity of prayer and action must come rather from the union of our will with God's will. God is constantly present and willfully working in each moment of our lives. We can unite our will with His will to do all for love and glory to Him.

St. Paul teaches us that we are to find God in all things and all things in God. The transfiguration of this material world will be this continuing contemplation of all things in God. This can never be conceived as pantheism, which doctrine holds that all things are God, that God absorbs all material creation into Himself so nothing will exist but God. But St. Paul rightfully insists that all creation will remain always God's creation, distinct from God the Creator, even in Heaven.

Our spiritual movement, therefore, both in our earthly pilgrimage and in the life to come, should not go from created things to the Creator, but always the Creator, Father, Son and Holy Spirit, toward creatures. We should find shining through creatures, the glory and majesty of Him without whom they are nothing. We can see that we and all other creatures ". . . live and move and have our being" (Ac 17:28) in God. We are to enter into God by fixing our heart on God and we must never leave Him, not even in action. Truth convinces us that God is truly the ground of all being. How could any creature exist without God's immanent presence sustaining it from within the creature itself? We seek both in prayer and in action to remain completely attached and submissive to the action of God as He leads the world toward His end.

We, the disciples of Christ, become God's living instruments, or, better yet, His "co-creators" as we become more and more submissive to His guiding hand in all we do. Our loving submissiveness gives us true freedom to take our life and our talents and freely offer them to our Divine Creator. Love fixed on God welcomes action because it recognizes action as a sharing in God's work. Our actions reveal His work in us. They make us love Him all the more.

The Discipline Of Work

Our loving devotion to God will consist of the kind of familiarity with God which will increase with work undertaken for His love. Our work in all details will find God as its beginning, middle and end. Fidelity to work will be our way of advancing the kingdom of God. Creatures will progressively reveal for us the glory of God, even as God intended them to do. We will find ourselves returning to Eden as we live in harmony with God's will and in loving service to the world around us.

By recognizing the action of God through us, and cooperating with this action, we will glorify Him in His creative work. This supernatural view of all things in God will make us understand human beings and created things more in their full splendor of creation. We will come to see fully that all things are given us to serve and glorify God. Thus we understand that everything is a gift of God and it is right to return it to Him. True devotion will grow within us. But this prayerful attitude will be developed only within action, since action alone reveals how God acts in His creatures.

Consistent devotion demands continual inner discipline. Devotion and discipline, contemplation and asceticism, are two faces of the same reality. No work, even undertaken for love of God or neighbor, is ever performed without becoming to some extent an occasion of egotistic satisfaction, sense pleasures of the body or mind. To purify yourself and heal the roots of self-centeredness comes about slowly. It occurs in successive stages which your action itself determines. You are plunged into a dangerous arena, not only dangerous from outside creatures acting upon and reacting to you, but dangerous because the given situation draws out the hidden areas of your bias toward self.

Such a situation is an occasion for you to enter into an interior combat, a purifying of yourself from the dross of selfishness, to allow the pure gold of love to come forth. Health will be given to you only in the therapy of conflict and pain. Thus we see the importance of staying inside any given situation and not turning outwardly to diversions that take us away from the battle. We stay at the work at hand and there purify our intentions as we trust solely in God's strength, as we purify ourselves to work only for His glory.

Thus union with God by action becomes at the same time a devotion and an inexhaustible source of asceticism. If our understanding demands our whole concentration, we should rejoice in it as an interior struggle, the cross, that goes to the very root of self. Those who fear action without discipline are far from attaining the desired purity to see God. They truly resist God. But true fidelity consists in constantly using all our powers in order to help us to find God and at the same time subdue ourselves.

The discipline is not an end in itself but it brings about the inner purification that will fully transform our wills into a oneness with God's will. This brings about the fruit of pure love that frees us to possess all things in God as we renounce all selfishness or self-love. Our prayer gradually ceases to be so many individual acts, but rests finally and firmly fixed on God, even at the height of greatest activity and struggle. Action and prayer, then, tend to become a single activity. They cannot be separated. When we will to cooperate with God's plan of creation, redemption and sanctification, we become absorbed into a given work which charity commands by the love of God who lives in us. We lose ourselves in the stream of this love as it flows through our creative work done in oneness with God's creative Word. With our intentions clarified by faith, hope and love, we lovingly take our places in the vineyard of the Lord and labor all day with serene confidence because we know that the Master will remain with us until evening comes.

Contemplation to Obtain Divine Love

If you have ever made a retreat based upon St. Ignatius' *Spiritual Exercises*, you will be familiar with the beautiful, final contemplative consideration which he proposes to the retreatant to help him/her to return to daily life and live as a contemplative in action. We can best summarize what has been said in this teaching by outlining the features of this consideration.

St. Ignatius always begins and ends with God who is love (1 Jn 4:8). Love is always a movement that explodes from the depths of a person's being to share that being with another. God moves outwardly from within the trinitarian community of love to communicate Himself to us human beings unto communion. Love needs an external expression. Love is proved, is enfleshed, and truly becomes love by deeds. Faith without deeds is dead (Ja 2:17).

Creative action best communicates love given. But such creative action admits of several levels of self-giving as being "present" to the one loved.

1. The first way that God wishes to be present to you is through the created gifts which He gives you. His beauty and infinite perfections are mirrored in the limited perfections of His creatures. When you reflect upon all the gifts you have received from God and are now receiving, you respond to God's presence in His gifts by praising and thanking Him for His gratuitous expressions of His love for you.

We think of some of these great gifts that God so constantly pours out upon us. There is the gift of ourselves, in all our uniqueness. This embraces the gifts of our parents, our existence, our health, our body, soul and spirit. We have been made in God's image and likeness through our ability to think, know and love. We have received and are receiving at every moment innumerable gifts that are unique to ourselves. Included in these gifts are the gift of our Christian faith, the Eucharist, the charisms of the Holy Spirit, the gift of loving friends. What is our response to God who communicates Himself to us through His gifts? We should walk through life thanking God for all things, even the trials, for we praise God for His constant love working to direct all things unto good if we love Him (Rm 8:28).

2. Yet God wishes to be even more present to us by being *inside* of each gift. He is not merely content to give Himself to us in extrinsic gifts, but He wishes to be present to us in the very gifts that we receive from Him. Everything we touch, therefore, should be an occasion to touch God who is immanently present in His gifts to us. "Where could I go to escape your spirit? Where could I flee from your presence?"(Ps.139:7).

What should be our response to God's presence inside all of His gifts? It should be *reverence*. Creatures should not take us away in our working hours but actually should be the occasion to experience God even more present to us within the gifts. As we touch each created gift from God, we touch God's holy presence. We move in an atmosphere of reverent awe at God's all pervasive, loving presence everywhere. Each place in which we find ourselves becomes holy for us.

3. God wishes still more to be present to us in His self-giving love. If love is proved by deeds, then God is working inside of each gift He gives you. He works for you in order that He may share Himself with you, making you "a participator of God's very own nature" (2 P 1:4). God is most present to you as He is working constantly in each moment and in each creature (Jn 5:17) to allow you to receive Him in loving union.

What is your response to God who is "laboring" and has been laboring since the beginning of material creation to provide you with all you need to develop into the unique, loving person He always has loved in His Son? Your response is to do everything in your daily work for love of God; but now you realize that God is living within you and in the material which you touch and work over. The two of you are working to fashion the total Christ, the Body made up of this material world which has its fullness of being in God's Word, Jesus Christ.

A Prayer Exercise

In the presence of the living Trinity abiding within you, stretch out your hands and ask God to fill them with His energies of love. Beg Him to use your weaknesses in order that His glory may appear to you in each event. May you have new eyes to contemplate Jesus Christ, shining "diaphanously" (in Teilhard's term) in each moment of your material existence and in each creature you encounter. Cry out in pain that Jesus Christ be brought forth in glory. Offer your hands and lips to be channels of the healing power of Christ among His people again. God is at the heart of the matter. You are to become a contemplative in action!

Learn that your life, your work is to praise God in His gifts; to be present to God in reverence as you discover Him in all things; above all, work with Him Who is working inside of each event, that Christ be brought forth so that you, with the risen Jesus and His Spirit of love, can be a *praise*, *reverence* and *service* out of returned love to Him who is Love itself.

Chapter Eight:

PRAYING WITH YOUR WHOLE BEING

We are all quite aware that we stand on the threshold of a new awakening. Social, economic and religious forms we have lived by no longer seem adequate to answer our problems and our inner cravings for greater global unity. Everything around us in our society and church is being challenged. Old patterns, once useful, have been discarded. New forms have not always been found to replace the old and there is often a great vacuum in our lives, bringing forth much undue stress and anxiety.

Traditionalists call us back to the "tried and the true." Yet most of us long for a more dynamic process of evolution, relational energies, stirred up into a "mix" of awesome richness which can allow new forms to come forth in answer to the challenges given to us modern beings.

We need to move away, especially in our religious outlooks, from a static, mechanistic and legal view of reality to discover a holistic approach, through personal integration of the diverse but not separate elements that make us up, to become who we are being called to be by God's constant, active presence as Love.

Praying with our whole person is an attempt to unite our body, soul and spirit within ourselves when we pray, and outside of ourselves when we relate through our creative work to the world of other human beings and all material creation. It is a challenge to break away from the deadly trichotomy that pits our human body against our soul against our spirit. It is a call to quiet each level of our being into a new wholeness in order that we may go deeper into the center of our being and release the powers of creative love to bring forth a better world.

Praying With Your Whole Being

You are, in a very real way, everything you see, hear, touch, taste and smell. The years of living in and through your senses have added up to make you *you*. Your psychic life, your heredity, years of living in and through your emotions and passions, of which the two strongest are love and hate, all have added up to make you *you*. But these various levels of *your* being keep you in the area of the "many", of multiplicity, potentiality unto a unity that alone will give you full meaning. You sense in your daily living, and even in your moments of deep aloneness with God in prayer, that you are being acted upon by objects, that you are not really *you* in a oneness, in a unity, in the all-mastering creativity whence you can rise and dominate, and as a self-directing agent, choose your own destiny.

Part of the disunity in divine-human relationships comes from our separation (at least in our thinking) of our bodies and souls from themselves. As long as we perceive ourselves as disjointed, we will live in a fragmented, non-holistic manner toward the world around us, toward other human beings and toward God. God created us as whole persons. We are not made up of several parts, put together with some invisible glue!

In the Bible we are given a vision of the human being as a unified, whole person in relationships with fellow-human beings, with God and with the entire created, material world. Through modern biblical research, theologians such as Karl Rahner, Paul Chauchard and many others have sought to present the human person in terms of body, soul and spirit relationships, a view, they feel, as more consonant with the concept of man and woman as presented by writers of the Bible. St. Paul captures this holistic view when he describes a human person in a process of becoming holy and blameless, "spirit, soul and body, for the coming of our Lord Jesus Christ" (1 Th 5:23).

In the Old Testament man is not seen as possessing a life-giving soul, but he becomes a living soul. Man receives such an inner source of life from God "breathing into his nostrils a breath of life" (Gn 2:7) which affects the whole of man's well-being. It is a rich concept that stresses the oneness in all human beings. The Jewish mind could never separate us from our souls or from our bodies. We are an "ensouled" being and an "embodied" being as well as an "enspirited" being. Flesh and spirit describe different relationships of us to God, as transient creatures relating to God, yet as total beings, formed and strengthened by God's loving presence or spirit. God has placed within our bodies a basic rhythm, an inner harmony among all parts of the body, the organs, nerves, muscles and so forth. When such harmony is attained and lived out, it leads the human person to an integration of higher faculties found in the psyche and the spirit.

Turning Within

In order to move away from sheer multiplicity without any unity we need to turn inwardly to discover, at the center our being, the unifying Spirit of God's love. It is only in the Spirit of love experienced in a personalized, deep prayerful encounter, often renewed each day, that you and I can enter into the Source of our being and find peace and joy and ongoing integration and wholeness. True healing and wholeness come from the center of our being, where we enter once we have closed the door of our inner closet (Mt 6:6) and excluded any disintegration from our sense and psychic experiences.

Take the familiar example of a lake. It is most acted upon or readily changed on its surface. Pass down through the various levels of water, always descend into purer water, leave the disturbances on the surface far behind, experience deeper and deeper quiet, and you begin to touch the source that feeds the whole lake. Here, there is the purest activity without multiplicity, a minimum of activity. We need to experience daily this turning within ourselves if we are to pray as we ought, in the Spirit who comes to help us in our weakness (Rm 8:26-27). It is in the depths of our being that we will find the image according to which God has made us. Here are the "living waters that flow into eternal life" (Jn 7:37). Here we are truly ourselves, in complete freedom, capable of saying *yes* or *no* to the Heavenly Father.

Jans Ruysbroeck, the 14th century Flemish mystic, has an apt quotation: "You know well that a meeting is a gathering of two persons coming from different places which in themselves are opposite and apart. Now, Christ comes from above as a lord and generous donor who can do all things. We come from below (from earth) as poor folk, devoid of strength and in need of everything. Christ comes in us *from within outwards, and we come to Him from outside inwards.* And for this reason, a spiritual meeting must here take place."

Having made yourself open to Him who contains all things, you now experience the most natural "stretching" forth, returning through your psychic world to the surface of your "lake" to enter again the world of multiplicity. Now there is no longer a oneness in which *you* pit yourself against others outside yourself. The community of yourself, being in oneness with God, established within the depths of your being now allows you to move in union with God to carry your microcosmic oneness, your loving community, grounded in God's triune presence, into the separated world outside of you.

Your "worldly" activities are the food for your community, both with God and your neighbor. They are the raw stuff for your choices whereby your faith, hope and charity grow from intellectual acts into intuitional experiences, whereby the many objects outside of you and even within your total makeup, not losing their "manyness," are molded into a symphonic whole. The diversity of parts is always present, yet the unifying force of God's Spirit always gives you the realization of a total "oneness" which you strive to actualize with God's cooperation.

New Ways of Praying

When we study the writings of spiritual authors, we see that the need for a constant searching of ways of praying has always been recognized by them. Many Christians have been unable to deepen their prayer life beyond a certain point in spite of their belief in their call to full union with God. There is also a need for a variety of methods for each individual, as St. Teresa suggests:

> Rigidity of any kind is to be avoided, for a certain variety in one's prayer whets the appetite. 'Sometimes do one thing, sometimes another, so that the soul will not get bored with always eating the same food,' (Life XIII). 'There is only one rule, to pray as one can' (The Way of Perfection, XXI)

Fr. Johannes Lotz, S.J. also remarks: "Methods should never be allowed to do violence to our individuality, but they should be used to free it and adapt it for the work of meditation so that each meditator can find his own way."

Hinduism has felt the same need and has developed several kinds of Yoga exercises to fit different types of personalities and to offer various ways to reach the Supreme Being. The Buddhist tradition has worked out a methodology using the whole body and the psychic powers. We Christians have inherited a tradition that has rather developed ways of using the Scriptures that appeal mostly to our reasoning faculties. Yet we find in the Bible this command: "You shall love Yahweh your God with all your heart, with all your soul, with all your strength" (Dt 6:5). And we hear Christ quoting this command in the Gospels. In other words a Christian in prayer should not only try to recollect his/her intellect, but also one's whole being. We should not only help ourselves with the reading of the Bible and using the imagination to bring us into the presence of God through Jesus Christ, but we should also learn to use our body to bring about in ourselves an integration of a whole person praying before God.

Progress In Prayer

Let us briefly describe the early stages of interior prayer since mystics agree that everyone has to go back to them from time to time. The first methods offered to Western beginners are mostly discursive meditation, the breath-prayer and a simple phrase meditation given by St. Ignatius in his second and third methods and the *lectio divina*, so well described in the Benedictine form of monastic prayer. Such a lectio prayer is done in three phrases: the reading of the Word, the personal appropriation of this Word in a concrete, contemporary and meaningful way to the individual, and the personal response of the meditator. The text chosen can be long or short. When it is short it can lead to affective prayer through the repetition of the same words.

Little by little the meditator should normally be led to the stage of affective prayer and even of the prayer of simplicity. Herbert Smith describes this latter simplication of our prayer:

> Our mind, will and affections have really been caught up in the mystery of Jesus. Our minds are steadier now because steady gazing on one truth is bringing such great rewards . . . . The intellect is at long last finding what the inner man really

wants, and even the senses are at times flooded with joy in response to these interior experiences.

This is considered a door to contemplative prayer. Let us see how we can use the body to enter more fully into such a simplified prayer. All mystical traditions of East and West agree that a certain amount of exterior silence is necessary at all levels of concentration inwardly. A certain amount of "aloneness" with the Alone is necessary. But true silence must move into an integration of all the powers of body, psyche and spirit if there is to be a true listening to God's inner Word. And how we Westerners need inner silence in order to reach that still-pointedness that all mystics speak of!

Yogic Concentration

Thousands of years before the advent of Christianity, Hindu Sannyasa hit upon the lotus position as one giving maximum relaxation and integration of body and spirit. The cross-legged sitting can be done in several ways according to the ability of the individual. Whatever position is chosen: lotus, half-lotus, or even sitting on a chair, one must make certain that the back is kept straight. The Zen masters of Buddhism recommend to keep the eyes half opened and to gaze. The hands are kept on top of one another on the lap. One has to find out by himself/herself which way of sitting and holding one's hands are the best. What is important is that one's body should be relaxed and comfortable but wide awake and inwardly attentive. Krishna advises Arjuna in the *Baghadvad Gita*: "Being seated there, making the mind one-pointed and subduing activities of mind and senses, let him practice Yoga for self-purification." This is what the Eastern Christian mystics called "pushing the mind into the heart."

A way of becoming "one-pointed," suggested by Yoga, is to look intently upon a flower, a painting or some object of beauty. Focus upon it with all your senses. Try to devour it with your eyes. Listen to the music of its colors. Smell its special fragrant beauty. Become immersed into the object so that soon the distance between you and the object is overcome and you feel one with the object contemplated. Gradually, a feeling that admits of great intensity and growth allows you to transcend the tyranny of your "conditioned" self and the limitations of place, time and uncontrolled desires.

Through such disciplined concentration you will not only begin to perceive a oneness with the world outside you but also a slowing down of your mental activities with an accompanying sense of deep peace and quiet.

Breathing and Relaxation

Breathing properly is the fundamental first step to uniting the powers of the body and soul into a totally, integrated person. It is absolutely necessary for periods of concentration such as study and formal prayer. Rhythmic breathing before entering upon such periods tends to make ourselves detached, relaxed and hence more free to reflect and focus our attention steadily, calmly and effortlessly on a given idea or in Christian prayer upon the indwelling Lord.

Let us study for a moment what is called abdominal breathing or diaphramatic breathing. We see the proper breathing done when a baby is sleeping quietly. Adults, through tension, introduce obstacles to this process. The pattern is: to fill the lungs from the abdomen. The upper chest usually does not move, except in full lung expansion. It is the abdomen that in normal, calm breathing expands and retracts and in this process the inhaled air is forced into the middle and upper chest. To facilitate diaphramatic breathing the following exercises can be performed. Try in the beginning to be aware of the movement of the air as it circulates through the thorax or chest region.

1. Standing by an open window, take a deep breath and observe the expansion in the region of the abdomen and at the sides and in back. Place the palms of your hands upon the lower ribs in the back and feel the expansion of the body

in this part pressing upward through the action of the diaphragm as a deep breath is inhaled. Try several deep inhalations and feel the rhythmic movement of the diaphragm muscle as it pushes outward and upward forcing the air into the chest region. As you breathe in deeply, feel the diaphragm muscle push outward. As you exhale, feel it move inward.

2. Seated with back straight up, do the "square" breathing. Breathe in four phases keeping an equal duration for each phase; e.g. for four beats simply breathe in; hold for four more; exhale for four and then hold for another four beats. Then begin again. Notice the rhythm and the calmness that is introduced into the body.

3. Now close the right nostril with the right thumb. Breathe in deeply and without strain through the left nostril, counting from one to three as you inhale. Shut the left nostril keeping the right also shut. Hold your breath as you count without rush to twelve. Keeping the left nostril shut, release the right and breathe out, counting up to six at the same speed. Then breathe in again through the same nostril, counting to five. Close it and hold your breath for twelve counts. Do about five such cycles, beginning and ending with the left nostril. The count is: 3:12:6. A sense of fullness, calmness should permeate your whole being.

Prostration

A form of body-prayer almost lost to Westerners is that of prostration. The lying on the floor, face down, fosters a great awareness of one's creaturehood. The body is completely opened, exposed, defenseless. The deep connection between openness, truth and simplicity is tangibly felt. It seems that the empirical *ego* runs away and there is only the true self left. One realizes that there is not much difference between one's self and the floor: only a group of chemical substances one upon another. For four senses the only contact with the world is through the floor and one feels amost one with it. The only sense which can act normally is the hearing, but all it can tell is that life is going on around it without it. All that one possesses is of no use: objects cannot be manipulated, talents cannot be used, no activity can be performed. This is a great help to maintain the person in a deep passive attitude.

This powerlessness brings forth the need to lose oneself in the Absolute, to surrender completely to God in order to be taken up by Him and be transformed into Him. A Christian can thus become more aware of God's active presence in everything and surrender one's whole being and especially one's will to Him. If you extend your arms sideward in the form of a cross, the experience becomes even more acute. Some quotations from Scripture may spring up from the unconscious and reveal their deep meaning:

> My heart has said of you,
> 'Seek his face,'
> Yahweh, I do seek your face;
> do not hide your face from me(Ps 27:8-9).

> Lovingly intervene, give me life (Ps 119:88).

> The spirit of the Lord, indeed, fills the whole world
> . . . holds all things together (Wi 1:7).

> For now your creator will be your husband (Is 54:5).

I would like to point out that, whereas the prostration gives an awareness of nothingness before the Absolute, the sitting position makes one more aware of the unifying process taking place in one's deep self. For a Christian believer the prostration makes the transcendence of God more tangible, whereas the sitting position makes His immanence more felt. In prostrating, one will be more conscious of his/her need for purification and of the role that God can play in this redemptive work. In sitting, the detachment seems to take place more by itself.

A Personal Experience of the Jesus Prayer

I would like to share with you a simple breathing prayer formed around the well-known Jesus Prayer, that is so much a part of Eastern Christian prayer. Perhaps it can open you to your own form of prayer that combines the elements of your body, soul and spirit relationships in an integrated prayer of deep personalism between you and Jesus Christ.

I begin by uttering only the word LORD. Each word of this prayer which I shall pronounce, one after the other, slowly, until I have completed the whole phrase, is a living experience of the indwelling Jesus. After each word, I shall pause to contemplate its significance. The first word, "Lord," is an appeal, a sigh from the soul, an ejaculation.

And now I say: LORD JESUS! I speak the name of my Lord. I call Him by His own name, His sweet and tender name. Now I direct my sighing toward the name and presence of Jesus. My sigh is fulfilled in His name and presence. If I go to the depths of my sigh, I discover the presence of Jesus within me.

Then I add the word: CHRIST. "Lord, Jesus Christ." My interior discovery deepens. I have found my Jesus as the intimate friend of my soul. Now a new experience reveals Him to me as the Christ. It concerns His function, His mission, His universal ministry. No longer is He simply intimate to me. He belongs to God, to all human beings. He exists for the whole of humanity and so do I. I contemplate the Incarnation.

I say again, "Lord, Jesus Christ!" and add SON OF GOD. I repeat, "Son of God, Son of God." These words lead me to the Holy Trinity. By the Son I go to the Father. I go also to the Holy Spirit who is the bond and union of the Father and the Son.

I now come to a new term: HAVE MERCY. My sigh had been lifted very high, even to the mysteries of the Incarnation and the Trinity. These words are an audacious cry. A door through Jesus is opened to me into God's heart, filled with divine pity and forgiveness and mercy. I unleash the spring and flow of the living waters which is the divine mercy. I repeat: "Have mercy!" that on me, on all, these waters may flow forth.

ON ME . . . . for such are the words which I now add: "Lord, Jesus Christ, Son of God, have mercy on me!" By these words I direct on to myself the torrent of divine mercy. I place myself, so to speak, under the fall of this flood of mercy. I am the subject of this infinite mercy. Jesus sees me and extends to me His mercy.

I speak now the last word of the Jesus Prayer and with this last word the prayer is completed: LORD, JESUS CHRIST, SON OF GOD, HAVE MERCY ON ME, *A SINNER!* Here then is the last word: "a sinner!" My interior gaze has turned from the divine glory, beyond the Incarnation and the Trinity and I see myself as a sinner. It is a fall from heaven to earth, even below the earth. I am plunged into the darkness of a soul deprived of God. A chasm divides me from God. This is not the final note. This is a movement of humility and repentance. As soon as I have spoken the whole phrase, I begin again slowly, word by word. This is an example of praying in the body, praying with the total powers of the physical, psychic and spiritual, which God has put into you. This is to pray holistically in an integration of yourself; into a one person encountering God as a oneness and the two of you becoming the ONE.

Chapter Nine:

STRESS, INNER PEACE AND HEALING

Jesus Christ is still the Prince of Peace who comes into our darkened world as Light. He comes as Divine Physician to heal us in our broken relationships with God, our neighbors, our world. We cry out for His coming to bring us into a new era of peace, joy and happiness.

Yet as Christians we know He is always abiding within us and working dynamically around us at all times. It is we who have to receive Him in the cave of our hearts. We are the ones who have to be born into His life.

Is your life becoming progressively more and more stressful? We are literally destroying our God-given health of body, soul, spirit by the excessive anxieties and stress under which we work, live and try to gain much-needed rest in nervous sleep. If Jesus Christ lives within us, it is for us to surrender ourselves to His infinite love for us. We need to pray more deeply and come into contact with His living love that drives out all fear (1 Jn 4:18).

Stress, Inner Peace And Healing

Most medical doctors would recommend to you, for almost all illnesses from the flu to heart attack, rest and silence. Our bodies are factories of tremendous energy and self-healing forces. Yet our Western culture seems to make the recommended rest and silence almost impossible to attain, since the demands of such a culture produce pressure, tension and stress. Our time is spent competing for money, power and self-glorification. To relieve some pressure, we consume mammoth quantities of aspirins, antacids, tranquilizers and pep pills. We rush to psychiatrists to spill out our tensions and fears verbally, ever seeking release.

We are not a healthy people, and the root cause is the *stress* under which most of us live. We do not experience the inner silence which brings healing to our bodily and psychological tensions and anxieties because we seldom touch our indwelling, loving God, the Ground of our being.

Americans annually spend $120 million on laxatives alone. In one year we consume 5,000 tons of aspirin. Tons of sleeping pills, tranquilizers, reducing pills and antacids are consumed, in the attempt to cover up symptoms and messages from a suffering, noisy body, flogged mercilessly by a disturbed psyche. One half million die of heart attacks while 27 million have some kind of heart condition. Over 7 million people have some form of arthritis or rheumatism. One out of every ten men has a stomach ulcer. Millions suffer from diabetes or hypoglycemia, chronic disorders such as asthma, anemia, multiple sclerosis, cancer, senility, mental and nervous diseases, alcoholism and respiratory difficulties. Twenty-five percent of Americans have the problem of obesity.

Stress

What is stress? Usually we refer to the everyday wear and tear on the mind and body as stress. Dr. Hans Selye, the leading authority of stress, gives it an exact, scientific meaning. He defines stress as "the body's non-specific response to any demand made upon it." Thus, stress refers to the uniform set of changes that occur throughout your body whenever you meet any external or internal demand, be it physical or emotional.

You might be "stressed" because of an argument in your family or at work, or because of a viral infection, or a worry about your finances. Whatever the source physical or psychological, stress always produces some bodily changes. Some of these are muscular tension, increased heart rate, accelerated breathing, mild to profuse sweating, cold hands or feet and anxiety. If such effects endure for a long time, a battery of chemical changes takes place within your body.

Some of the symptoms of excessive stress are: feeling worn out at the end of the day, difficulty in falling asleep or sleeping through the night, tension headaches, free-floating anxiety, feeling "all-wound-up," feeling depressed, pouches or dark circles under the eyes, worries, inability to concentrate, irritability, frequent indigestion, constipation and colds, frequent angry outbursts, excessive drinking, smoking and eating.

Stress Response

Dr. Hans Selye discovered the stress response more than three decades ago. He observed that the central nervous system registers a demand on your physical-emotional-spiritual resources. The demand might be caused by an argument with a loved one or a reaction to a disobedient child, or to loud noises around you.

The first stage is the *alarm* stage. This triggers off, within the autonomic nervous system, a "fight or flight" syndrome. This is a surge of energy produced by the release of adrenaline from the adrenal glands. Energies are mobilized in order to attack or flee from the impending "enemy"—that person or event that is seen as a threat to our safety. The heart beats faster, breathing accelerates and muscles become tensed and ready for action.

This first stage of stress response is not bad in itself. It often has saved our lives or the lives of others. It fuels excitement for pleasures and increases anger in frustrating situations. When the demanding situation passes, we normally are "exhausted" and naturally need to restore our inner integration by "recharging our batteries."

If, however, the demanding situation is not resolved, and fear, worry or frustration remain, we enter into the second phase of stress. Again, this is not necessarily a bad reaction for it allows us to enter into the stage of resistance in the case of an extended illness or imprisonment etc. On this level of stress we find a prolonged high level of adrenaline pumped into the system along with other hormones necessary for long-term resistance.

The normal stage that follows this second stage of stress response is again exhaustion. On this level, if we do not have rest, fatigue will continue and serious effects, destructive to our well-being, will result. Some of these effects are: chronic elevation of blood pressure with slow but steady damage to heart, kidneys and the entire cardiovascular system; tearing of arterial walls and increased plaque formation (clogging) in the arteries; increased blood sugar levels which raise cholesterol levels; lowered resistance to disease through a reduction in certain critically important white blood cell levels; increased stomach acidity and changes in the stomach lining which contribute to gastrointestinal distress and ulcer formation; increased inflammation in joints, aches and pains, and ultimately chronic arthritis; hyperactivity of the entire system, resulting in mental-physical exhaustion, chronic fatigue and insomnia.

Jesus The Divine Physician

Is there any hope or way by which we can offset the ravages of stress in our lives? We Christians believe in God's infinite love for each of His children, especially in the healing power given to His Son, Jesus Christ. We believe that Jesus went about healing all the sick persons brought to Him, provided they believed in Him.

Jesus was in touch with His Father's uncreated energies in a way that no other human being ever has been. God created man's psyche in such a way that the unconscious, receiving a suggestion from an outside authority, can unleash great energies effecting healings and miraculous actions normally not performed by man on a conscious level.

Use Of Techniques

Jesus used matter. He made a paste of spittle and clay and laid it on the blind man's eyes and told him to bathe his eyes in the Pool of Siloam (Jn 9:6-7). He put spittle on the eyes of the blind man at Bethsaida and laid His hands on him and after two attempts He healed him (Mk 8:22-26). The woman with a hemorrhage touched Him and He felt a current of energy pass from Him to her. His Disciples were instructed by Him to anoint with oil, and healings were effected (Mk 6:13).

Jesus often gazed intently upon a sick person in need of healing as did Peter and John in healing a cripple at the Gate Beautiful (Ac 3:4). Jesus often gave the suggestion, asking whether the sick wanted to be healed and whether they believed firmly that they would be healed. Using such techniques, Jesus allowed the sick person the opportunity to become attentive to God's presence in Him. Jesus was the concrete expression of God's love for His sick children. By His gaze, touch, His whole gentle presence, Jesus opened the sick to the inner depths of God's presence within them. They yielded in faith to God's mysterious presence within Jesus that released God's loving, healing presence in themselves.

Jesus was telling them that on all levels the Heavenly Father was concerned and wanted them to be healthy, if they would yield to that inner divine power locked within them. His Spirit of love allows us to see and experience by faith His presence as the Father's love, living within us and He calls us into healing unto abundant life. As we are healed on all levels: spirit, soul and body relationships, we are called out to be channels of God's healing love to each person we meet. It is God's love in us that heals us and allows others to be healed by our touch, our look, our word.

Techniques In Prayer

If the Trinity dwells within us, how can we tap into that healing power of God's love? We should not fear using techniques of centering ourselves in God's presence so that we may submit our tensioned fears to the perfect love of God. We have always maintained a healthy use of material techniques in bread and wine, oil, holy water in the sacraments. Should we, therefore, fear techniques for becoming quieted, techniques that we can find employed by all human beings, regardless of country and religion? Man universally the world over has learned to calm his psychic inner world by a rhythmic breathing. The body, soul and spirit merge into a relaxed "whole" person as God's breath is followed inwardly and outwardly, back and forth. One can concentrate on a burning candle and be powerfully aware of Jesus Christ as the light of the world. Or one gazes lovingly at a scene of nature, a picture or statue, or at the tabernacle that contains the Blessed Sacrament. One finds a reposeful and deeply prayerful attitude coming over him-herself. Churches have always realized the powerful technique of music in church services to quiet the participants and open their deeper selves to prayerful worship.

Such fixation points pull our dispersion to a centering-point so that our hearts can move easily to contemplate the transcendent God as immanently present within us. The ultimate worth of any technique must be measured by the fruit produced. A technique has no meaning unless we ask the question: "How is it being used? What are the fruits that come from such use? Does it help us or others to pray with greater consciousness, beyond the habitual, superficial level of controlled, discursive prayer?"

The Jesus Prayer

We Catholics have had a long tradition, both in the East and the West, of breathing in the name of Jesus in order to experience His healing power as an indwelling, risen Lord. The early Christians, as we read in Acts, knew by faith and experience that there was no other name whereby they would be healed and saved (Ac 4:12). Gradually a Christian mantra was developed in the Christian East which monks of the desert recited day and night: "Lord, Jesus Christ, Son of God, have mercy on me, a sinner!"

Thus a true transcendental meditation developed from the earliest centuries of Christianity. It was not "imported" from Hinduism. The unerring instincts of the Christian athletes of the desert, led by the Spirit, developed the *Jesus Prayer*. It was more than a technique. It was a summary of the whole Gospel that God so loved this world (Jn 3:16) as to give us His only begotten Son who died for love of us but rose from the dead in order to dwell within us. Through His released Spirit of love, we Christians can experience the deepest silence, the richest healings by surrendering to His perfect love.

Their faith told them that He who was within them was greater than any other force without (1 Jn 4:4). The more they felt the healing power of Jesus Lord, the Divine Physician, the more they cried out in humility and poverty for continued healing and greater unity in Christ for themselves and for the whole human race.

Meeting The Lord In Darkness

Do you seek an answer, a way to deal with the stress and anxieties that hold you enslaved to dark powers that cripple your health in body, soul and spirit? The answer is Jesus Christ, the Way, the Truth and the Life (Jn 14:6). But the secret is to open yourself up deeply, both in quieted consciousness and in the deepest recesses of your dark unconscious, to His living and healing presence. This means that you can and should use techniques to quiet yourself on all levels of your being.

I would like to share with you how I learned to cope with stresses in my own life. Ask yourself whether God is calling you into deeper prayer and more intense silence through a similar method of encountering the healing Lord. While studying the Fathers of the desert, I saw how they broke their sleep to rise in a night vigil to worship God. There was always the element of waiting for the Parousia, the full coming of Christ, both in their own lives and in the entire world.

For over 25 years I have found this practice most helpful and health-giving. Praying at night, around 2 A.M. after three or so hours of refreshing sleep, brought me into a purer faith in the presence of Jesus Risen. The light of Christ is experienced as truly overcoming the powers of darkness and sin, not only in one's soul but also in the world. While the majority of people remain sleeping, a handful of Christians are waiting for the Bridegroom to come. In the middle of the night they cry out joyfully: "The bridegroom is here! Go out and meet him" (Mt 25:6).

During this treasured time, any anxieties or stress that filled the previous day are shed like water, as I am wrapped in the warming arms of my Savior.

Healing Love

Those who have accustomed themselves habitually to such nightly visits with the Divine Physician, have experienced a deep level of healing of hurts lodged deeply within the unconscious. This healing is known and experienced as new strength and loving power of creativity, are felt during the coming day. Concentration on daily tasks becomes much easier since the source of much distraction and diffusion, of fears and anxieties, has been dispelled by the enlivened consciousness of being grounded in God's light. "You are all sons of light and sons of the day" (1 Th 5:5). You might just like to experiment. Tell the Lord I sent you!

Chapter Ten:

CONTEMPLATION AND SELF-EMPTYING LOVE

To help you focus on the great self-emptying love of God toward you through the sufferings and death of His image, Jesus Christ, I have chosen the theme of the *kenotic*, or emptying, love of Jesus Christ. He is the human expression of the Trinity's great love for us. Both His love and that of the Trinity are measured by the Father, Son and Holy Spirit's outpouring, self-emptying gift of each Person to us. True love always is a *kenosis*, as St. Paul describes Christ's love for us in Philippians 2:6-11.

But both God's love for each other in the Trinity and for us, and our love in return to God and toward our neighbor are to be rooted in the "pass-over" experience of leaving a position of self-possession to live in loving service for others.

Jesus images God's love, and what our loving service should be like in His living for others in loving compassion. Love with compassion wishes to do all, to accept any and all sufferings, even death, in order to serve the goodness and happiness of another.

Contemplation and Self-Emptying Love

True love and genuine contemplation are not very much different from each other. Both demand a "pass-over" experience. In true love toward God or another human person and in deeper prayer we need to move away from our ego-centeredness and focus in utter availability and self-giving upon the other, be it God or loved one in a human relationship. Such love we can call "self-emptying."

St. Paul uses a most ancient Christian hymn to teach the Philippians how they are to be "self-emptying" in true love toward each other. He uses the Greek verb, *kenoo*, to mean simply "to empty" or also "to make void, of no effect."

> His state was divine,
> yet he did not cling
> to his equality with God
> but emptied himself
> to assume the condition of a slave,
> and became as men are;
> and being as all men are,
> he was humbler yet,
> even to accepting death,
> death on a cross.
> But God raised him high
> and gave him the name
> which is above all other names
> so that all beings in the heavens, on earth and in the underworld,
> should bend the knee at the name of Jesus
> and that every tongue should acclaim
> Jesus Christ as Lord,
> to the glory of God the Father (Ph 2:6-11).

I believe most of us have misunderstood this important text to imply merely that Jesus is the pre-existent, eternal Word of God, equal to the Father in His divine nature. He puts aside His powerful, omniscient divinity to take upon

Himself our weak humanity. The verb, "he emptied himself," has no object to tell us of what He has emptied Himself. He empties Himself as one pouring himself out.

Who Sees Me, Sees The Father

Such an interpretation seems to objectivize the two natures of Christ. We could erroneously consider His divinity as having been put aside and His humanity would exist almost with its own act of existence, separated and independent from His divinity. If Jesus Christ is the true image of the invisible God (Col 1:15), let us see this text as a true manifestation of what the Father is like and what truly constitutes the nature of love within the Trinity.

Precisely because Jesus Christ is in the form of God, "one with God," He lives out, in His incarnational form of the Word made flesh, the essence of God's true love. God is not God because He holds on to His life, always having His own way. He, through the incarnation of Jesus Christ, shows us that God is love by self-giving, by being gift to others.

Only by God's becoming a human being and living a life of self-giving, of self-emptying love as a suffering servant for all human beings, but especially the poor, the sick, the outcasts and the sinners, can we come to know the real nature of God as compassionate love. Now we know God is as Jesus lives. Jesus is not so much God because He performs superhuman miracles and healings worthy only of His omnipotence, but because he images God's self-emptying love for all His children.

Because Jesus is the image of God in human form, He shows this not by holding within Himself His power, but He shows Himself as non-grasping, unself-centered, as a servant to those in need. Emptiness is thus in God a filling up; giving away means truly possessing. Now "losing one's life" in love means to find it in a greater manifestation and enrichment.

All the human limitations mentioned in this letter to the Philippians were accepted by Jesus: human weaknesses, finiteness, temptations and even death. And this aceptance can be seen as a positive expression of His divinity, rather than a negation or curtailing of it. This is "God's foolishness (which) is wiser than human wisdom and God's weakness is stronger than human strength" (1 Co 1:25). God's glory is shown in shame and weakness, accepted as self-emptying love for us. God is divine, and also Jesus of Nazareth because the latter images the former in generous self-giving and not in self-centeredness.

Jesus—Friend Of The Outcasts

One word, for me, most adequately expresses Jesus' mirroring to us the passionate love God, the Trinity, has for us. That word is, *compassion*. It denotes an active "fellow-sufferer." It means that He took upon Himself the sufferings, pains, limitations and even sins of each of us out of love for us.

Jesus came among men and women, as gentle and kind. He told His followers that they were to give away their lives for love of one another. He was the "friend of sinners," and went about doing good to the consternation of the decadent religious leaders of His time. To any sick or disturbed person He brought comfort and healing. He was meek and humble and wanted no part of Caesar's power. The only power He possessed was love. He loved each person who came into His life with the love of God Himself. He touched the crowds, listened to their anxieties, forgave their sins. He lived only to bring life, and that most abundantly, to all who wanted it. He was totally available to anyone who needed Him.

He had few disciples because many thought He was *mad*. At least, like the rich young man (Mk 10:17-22), many walked away when he suggested the crazy idea that he who was wealthy should go and sell everything he had, give the money to the poor and follow Him.

He was the most "impractical" person. People were not to worry about what they ate or put on, but they were to seek only the Kingdom of Heaven. But then He didn't have a pillow to put His head on at night. His disciples were to love everyone, even those who hated them. But really! And then He insisted:

> . . . bless those who curse you, pray for those who treat you badly. To the man who slaps you on one cheek, present the other cheek too; to the man who takes your cloak from you, do not refuse your tunic. Give to everyone who asks you and do not ask for your property back from the man who robs you. Treat others as you would like them to treat you. If you love those who love you, what thanks can you expect? Even sinners love those who love them. And if you do good to those who do good to you, what thanks can you expect? For even sinners do that much. And if you lend to those from whom you hope to receive, what thanks can you expect? Even sinners lend to sinners to get back the same amount. Instead love your enemies and do good, and lend without any hope of return . . . Give and there will be gifts for you; a full measure, pressed down, shaken together, and running over, will be poured into your lap; because the amount you measure out is the amount you will be given back (Lk 6:28-38).

His language sounded extravagant, unreal and most impractical. If you had an eye that scandalized you, you were to gouge it out. If you really had faith, you could walk up to a mountain and tell it to jump into the sea and it would do just that.

We were to visit the sick, the lonely, those deadly murderers in prison and tell them that we loved them. We were to give and give, even losing our lives for others. We were to hate our parents, brothers and sisters, and follow only Him.

We were to be servants to everyone, washing their feet, binding up their wounds, meeting all their needs. For such God does!

And all that he asked of His followers, He did Himself. When He washed the feet of His disciples, He summarized who He was. He was *Ebed Yahweh*, God's servant, suffering for His people.

Jesus was conscious that everything He did came from His Father. He lived only to please Him and bring Him glory. Jesus reveals an inner consciousness of His ultimate worth and meaning as a human being that derives from His complete dependence on the Father. In deep prayer and great intimacy Jesus would experience the self-giving of His Father, pouring the fullness of divinity (Col 2:9) into His Son. In His human weaknesses and temptations, He experienced the compassionate love of the Father for Him. And so He strove to live as He experienced the living activities of the emptying, loving Father in His life.

The Suffering Servant

Jesus and His early disciples were aware that His whole mission in life was to serve the Father's will. But it was clear in the consciousness of Christ made more detailed as He met the unfolding will of His Father each moment of His earthly life, that His service to the Father was a service on behalf of God's children. That service to the Father was a service pushed to such self-forgetting that Jesus would be brought to a free gift of Himself on behalf of the human race. There developed in Jesus an urgency of necessity that eventually His service of compassionate love to mankind would be concretized when He, the Good Shepherd, would lay down His life for all human beings.

The *kerygma* or preaching of the early Church, as found in the Gospels and Pauline writings, clearly attests to the necessity of Jesus to serve unto humiliating death so that He might enter into glory. He Himself explained patiently to the two disciples on the road to Emmaus: "You foolish men! So slow to believe the full message of the prophets! Was it not ordained that the Christ should suffer and so enter into his glory?" (Lk 24:25-26).

In the Synoptic Gospels, Jesus is presented as predicting three times His humiliating death, indicating a certain necessity (Mk 8:31; MK 9:35, Mk 10:43-45). It is easy to see in these texts, describing Jesus as suffering servant, the prophetic descriptions in the four songs of Deutero-Isaiah (Is 42:1-9; 49:1-11; 50:4-11; 52:13-53:12).

We learn why Jesus gives pleasure to the Father. He has come to serve with godly compassion the despised ones of the earth, the broken ones, the marginalized in order that we can understand in human communication of actions unto death what God is truly like.

The Logic Of Love

I have often asked myself the question: "But why the cross?" Could God not have been equally pleased that Jesus as servant, merely lived in that lowly state as man? Even if a blood offering were man's most basic symbol of total giving, could not the human race have been redeemed by one drop from the Lamb of God? Why such a prodigality of emptying, to the point of complete dehumanization? Jesus empties Himself not only for His divine glory but goes further even to emptying Himself of all control over His human existence (cf.: Is 53:2-4).

The terrifying sufferings, His service on our behalf, especially in Gethsemane and on Calvary, cannot theologically be understood only by a legalistic theory of atonement. There must be more that the Word of God reveals to us in deep contemplation of Christ's sufferings, that only His Holy Spirit can reveal far beyond the reach of our intellect.

Just as our human love knows various degrees of acting out the love we have for another, so Jesus grew in His freedom to surrender Himself completely to the Father. One returns love to the degree that he/she is aware consciously of how much another loves him/her. Jesus, in His long hours of solitary communion with the Father, must have received progressively deeper and deeper assurances of the Father's infinite love for Him. If mystics could lose consciousness under the rapture of God's piercing love for them, what must Jesus have experienced as the burning fire of the Father's love for Him poured over Him filling Him with light, "Light from Light"?

As Jesus experienced in prayerful communion His Heavenly Father's immense love for Him, especially at His Baptism, the forty days alone in the desert, His all-night vigils on the mountaintop, during His public ministry, in the Garden of Gethsemane and in dying on the cross, He grew in His sensitivity to that love and what it was asking of Him by way of a self-emptying in return.

Love Means Self-Sacrifice

Can we not say, therefore, that Jesus, becoming the suffering servant of Yahweh, freely wants to suffer and be poured out as spilt wax only because he wanted His human mind to be the perfect reflection of the Divine Mind? His human consciousness was to become one with the consciousness of the Father. Jesus in His service to the world, entering into the very depths of sin and death and utter emptiness of self, was choosing humanly to be as God is in His self-emptying love toward Him. It was the most perfect plan of imaging the eternal love of the Father for you and me. We have no other way of knowing the Father but through the Son. Here we have the perfect expression in human language of the very being of God who is love by nature.

Contemplative Prayer Is Emptying Love

In our intimate prayer, grounded in ever-deepening faith, hope and love, we open up to God's burning love and compassion for us in our many weaknesses and failures. You can experience daily as St. Paul did: "For me He dies!" Such an experience leads you into the awesome presence of the heavenly Father as perfect holiness, beauty and love. You realize that you are *now* being loved by your infinitely loving Father through the service of the Suffering Servant of Yahweh, Jesus Christ.

Such a healing of your loneliness and self-absorption bursts the bonds that hold you imprisoned in your narcissistic prison. It begins a transformation of your life which is a process shown by service to others.

You learn to move away from yourself as the center of all your thinking and praying. You center more completely on Christ who leads you into the similar self-emptying love of the Father and Holy Spirit which He continues to show you as He did in the Gospel and, above all, in His death on the cross.

Contemplation begins when you let go of your control in prayer, stop your long-winded speeches, above all, cease looking for consolations. As you experience God's dynamic, self-giving to you, you open up and return yourself as a gift of self-emptying love. There is no need to do anything. You are being transformed into love and compassion.

As you go forth from such deep prayer, you strive to live in compassionate, self-giving love to all. Loving, humble service to all whom you meet is the sign of contemplation for they are the same thing: self-emptying love.